Authority
Abusers

Authority
Abusers

GEORGE BLOOMER

WHITAKER
HOUSE

AUTHORITY ABUSERS

ISBN: 0-88368-768-2
Printed in the United States of America
© 1995 by Whitaker House

Whitaker House
30 Hunt Valley Circle
New Kensington, PA 15068
Visit our web site: www.whitakerhouse.com
Library of Congress Cataloging-in-Publication Data Pending

1 2 3 4 5 6 7 8 9 10 11 12 / 09 08 07 06 05 04 03 02

Dedication

This book is dedicated to my wife, Jeannie Bloomer, who has given unselfishly to the building of the ministry and my two beautiful daughters, Jessica and Jennifer, who've graciously shared their father with so many for the building of the kingdom of God.

Table of Contents

Acknowledgments

I'd like to acknowledge all those who've emptied themselves for the purpose of ministry. As you perservere toward excellence in ministry, may the true essence of servanthood and godly authority be revealed and restored in your life through the revelation of the written word.

Chapter One

An Atmosphere of Abuse

And if anyone causes one of these little ones who believe in me to
sin, it would be better for him to be thrown into the sea with a
large millstone tied around his neck.
—Mark 9:41

It is subtle, often invisible to those who are involved, but as deadly to the spirit as carbon monoxide is to the body. Police officers get jail time for it and parents lose custody of their children for it, but it happens every day in thousands of churches and families across the world.

I'm talking about authority abuse.

Most people have no idea how hurtful and destructive authority abuse can be. It's a difficult thing to talk about, sometimes a complicated issue. As with other forms of abuse, though, we must admit there is a problem before we can change for the better.

Exactly what is this problem? Is authority itself bad, something that should be avoided at all costs? Of course not. The problem is not with authority or even the use of authority; it is with people who abuse those under them and call that abuse "authority." This is when spirits get crushed and lives get broken.

Authority abuse is sin, a perversion of something beautiful. Such perversion can happen in any realm of life. Sexual desire between a man and a woman, for instance, is a beautiful thing in the context of marriage; that's how God designed it to be. Sex between a man and a prostitute, however, is an ugly, dirty thing that degrades both the man and woman involved because it does away with the holy intimacy God intended as the focus of the marriage bed.

> Godly authority is protective, loving, honest, and—above all—liberating.

Similarly, godly authority is protective, loving, honest, and—above all—liberating while the abuse of authority usually hinges on deception—often both the abuser and the abused are deceived—and keeps people from God's love and the freedom of His truth. Authority abuse stands between God and man, and so it is a sin against the very body of Christ. By separating innocent, defenseless members from the head, which is Christ (see Colossians 1:18), authority abusers spiritually cripple those members, often permanently.

Only when we reject authority abuse can we embrace the authority God has designed to bless and prosper us. But that's getting ahead of the story.

An Atmosphere of Abuse ✠

A Parable

There were two brothers, fresh out of college in the Midwest, who began a start-up agricultural venture. One brother focused on farming, applying the latest technology and innovative strategies to produce several varieties of cattle feed. The other began breeding and raising beef cattle, using state-of-the-art methods to track the herd's health and make breeding decisions. He bought feed exclusively from his brother, and the two developed a complex, highly personalized, but very profitable kickback plan for dividing their income.

By the time the brothers reached middle age, both were moderately wealthy, with the strongest young minds and bodies doing the daily managerial work for their agricultural estates. The summer that their combined worth topped four and a half million, they turned off their cell phones, took their wives, and left for a hunting vacation in the Rockies. They set no return date, only telling their foremen, "We'll be back when we both get our elk."

A month went by, and they were still gone. A month and two weeks. Two months. After two and a half months, the brothers returned with mountain tans, coolers full of hearty steaks, and one impressively mounted elk head apiece. The brother who raised beef found the office empty—one of his staff members was on a small, well-earned family vacation, so the foreman was out on the range with the company helicopter, supervising the birth of twin calves. All the books were up-to-date, all the bills current. Profits were down slightly, but everything was running smoothly and the foreman had logged more hours of work than any of the other help.

The brother with the crop-producing business came home to a party in his honor—or, rather, a party in honor of the "summer-long vacation" the foreman had concluded his boss must be on. This was one of a series of drunken bashes the foreman hosted; workers were required to help entertain his friends (he called them "business contacts") with no overtime pay. The office was full of empty coffee cups and doughnut boxes from the days the foreman spent there while everyone else was in the field. Profits were higher than ever before—at least they would have been if it weren't for the expensive parties. No one had been given vacation time, and no employee bonuses had been issued for two and a half months.

Needless to say, the first foreman was given a respectable bonus and a few extra days of paid vacation for his dedication and honest management. The second foreman was served a summary pink slip and couldn't even talk his way into a job pitching hay bales on and off the trucks.

Chances are, you're not wondering why the second guy got fired. Nobody would protest, "But he made more money for the company!" More likely, you feel he got off easy because a person in his position is responsible for the well-being of other employees and should not spend company resources on his own recreation. This man's behavior not only hurt the people he was supposed to motivate, encourage, and provide for; it also undermined the goals he was driving them toward. (See Matthew 24:44–51.) This is a prime example of authority abuse in action.

Feed My Sheep

In John 21, Jesus told Peter how the church is to demonstrate Christ's love to His people:

> *When they had finished eating, Jesus said to Simon Peter, "Simon son of John, do you truly love me more than these?"*

An Atmosphere of Abuse

"Yes, Lord," he said, "you know that I love you." Jesus said, "Feed my lambs." Again Jesus said, "Simon son of John, do you truly love me?" He answered, "Yes, Lord, you know that I love you." Jesus said, "Take care of my sheep." The third time he said to him, "Simon son of John, do you love me?" Peter was hurt because Jesus asked him the third time, "Do you love me?" He said, "Lord, you know all things; you know that I love you." Jesus said, "Feed my sheep."
(John 21:15–17)

Jesus' message to Peter is clear: loving Him means caring for (*"feeding"*) His little ones (*"lambs"*). On the surface, the church seems to have remembered this. The manicured lawns, smiling faces, and open arms of greeting at church doors could be an inviting alternative to the rugged way of life offered in a society of corporate cataclysms and "survival of the fittest" mentality. People are looking for acceptance, stability, even guidance—ultimately, they're looking for God—and the church should be the end of this search.

Unfortunately, the glitzy showmanship and manipulative teaching of men who seek self-glorification rather than revealing the glory of God often obstruct the acceptance, stability, guidance, and love that people seek. Thousands of people avoid Christians and going to church because the only message they have ever heard is one of judgment, criticism, and performance-based love. Irresponsible leaders have made God's business—with its saving, grace-filled mission statement—infamous as a place of rigid rules and stiff membership requirements, consequently turning seekers away from the God who can fulfill them.

In my twenty-three years of preaching, I have seen the following played out hundreds of times: a girl rebels against her parents, and, for a time, nothing they do works to bring her under control. She winds up getting pregnant. Naturally, this jolts her to her senses; she returns to obeying her parents' rules and seeks to give her life back to God in repentance. It's a painful lesson, but at least she has learned it. She starts on her way to healing and renewal.

Then authority figures at her local church intervene. They declare her to be an example of "sin in the camp" and demand that she leave her family and the church. Her mother is exiled from the choir, and her father is forced to step down as a deacon, all because their family is "tainted with sin"—as if they were the Old Testament children of Israel living under the law of Moses!

I have to ask, "Where, in all of this, is the grace and forgiveness of Jesus Christ?" The answer is, "Nowhere." This is simply spiritual abuse and condemnation posing as godly authority; this is man enforcing rules that Christ never engineered. Time and again I have seen lives devastated by this kind of abuse until I simply have to cry, "Enough!"

A few years ago, there were some serious scandals in the leadership of the United States Navy. Several high-ranking officials betrayed the trust given to them, mishandling both the resources and people put under their care. The offenses were committed by only a handful of officers, while dozens—even hundreds—of loyal, honest men and women did their best to lead a strong and honorable branch of the armed services. It was inevitable, though, that people began associating the US Navy with corruption. The abuse of authority is a serious, deadly thing, and the trust that was broken outweighed generations of integrity and courage.

The same thing has happened in the American church, but we can't blame it on one or two famous televangelists as the Navy could point fingers at just a few officers. From small country parishes to metropolitan mega-churches, it's possible to find pastors who abuse their position. The controlling, graceless dictatorship of man-centered religion knows no race or creed, gender or geography. As a result, many stable Christian institutions, founded upon and continually following the Word of God, have been lumped together with the hypocritical, life-damaging minority. The Good News of Jesus Christ is continually hindered by self-proclaiming dictators in the guise of spiritual shepherds, who actually lead the sheep astray.

A gentleman once told me that his church had a total of 147 people at every service, including communion, baptismal services, and baby dedications. There were never more than 147 people, but never fewer. Always exactly 147.

I asked him what kind of church it was, and the ministry he described sounded fairly decent. He explained, though, that the people of the church were absolutely terrified of the pastor and his wife. Apparently, the pastor and the first lady of the church had a say in the day-to-day lives of every member—daily duties, the way families were run, household finances—everything.

"Dear God, please don't let the pastor find out that I sinned."

His story reminded me of my own experience growing up in church. As a young boy, I often prayed about my sins. But I did not worry about what God thought of them or of me! My prayer was this: "Dear God, please don't let the pastor find out that I sinned." Because he led a very dogmatic and legalistic church, I feared the pastor more than God and became terrified that maybe God would allow this man to know my personal thoughts and feelings without my sharing them.

Authority Abusers

It's been many years since I was a little boy, but situations like mine still exist. Even today, congregations are suffocating in the poisonous atmosphere of an abusive authority. Many people have experienced a leader trying to control them by citing so-called "biblical obedience." Too often (even once is too often!), a person submits himself to the abusive pastor or ministry leadership only to find out that he or she is being made a slave to the whims and personal convictions of that authority. This control often goes so far as to dictate when families should go on vacations, how long couples should wait to consummate their marriage, where a family's children should attend school...And, sadly, the list goes on.

Countless numbers of people have been hurt by the institution originally established to bring them healing. Thus, there are many who truly and wholeheartedly love God but have no regard for the organized church. Denominationalism, tradition, and authority abuse have left a bad taste in the mouths of congregation members who depended, trusted, and leaned on their leaders. Many pastors and leaders have become task masters over the lives of God's people instead of leaders of accountability and caring!

Satan's desire has always been to exalt his position above the throne of God. He seeks to turn the world against the church and the God who upholds it, and he will use any willing vessel to achieve these goals. Though the number of good pastors and good churches outnumber the horror-story inspiring, congregation-controlling dictators disguised as spiritual leaders, the enemy would like to magnify the few bad seeds to corrupt the entire institution as we know it.

How many people do you know who have totally turned their backs on the church and vowed never to step foot into another Christian facility again because they have been hurt? Even though many people use this as an excuse not to come to church, we cannot ignore those who have sincerely been badgered, mishandled, and wounded by ungodly ministry. It is now time for those of us in the body of Christ to break away from the man-made traditions and manipulative tactics of control that produce such wounds. But how can we prepare the road to recovery for those who've been injured, while simultaneously opening the eyes of others to help them avoid the same traps?

After my childhood pastor died, years after I had grown up and begun my own ministry, God began revealing to me just how deep was the darkness that had surrounded my former pastor's church. God took me through a season of mental and spiritual purging during which my eyes were opened so that I would not unconsciously incorporate those same ungodly tactics into my own ministry. In short, God began removing the mental barriers—put up by my responses to this abusive authority—that were preventing me from knowing God as He really is. The more I understood about what true spiritual authority should look like and how this pastor had deviated from that truth, the more of I understood of God's character.

> How can we prepare the road to recovery for those who've been injured?

Now I know that it is only when we reject authority abuse that we can embrace the authority God has designed to bless and prosper us.

PART 1

What Good Is Authority?

Chapter Two

Godly Authority

God blessed them and said to them, "Be fruitful and increase in
number; fill the earth and subdue it. Rule over the fish of the sea
and the birds of the air and over every living creature
that moves on the ground."
—Genesis 1:28

The first house Jeannie and I built was in a mostly undeveloped area without many nearby houses. After the land had been perked and all the testing done, we formulated a site plan and thought we were well on our way to building an honest-to-goodness house. To our amazement, though, we were soon billed $50,000 to lay the foundation and connect sewage and water pipes to the city of Durham! This meant $50,000 of our money was going into the ground before any piece of the house's structure was even visible. Eventually the house was built, and we furnished it and moved in. As years passed, though, the foundation and whole house began settling; soon problems with the house's underground mechanics began to surface. Before it was all over we had to dig four feet below the foundation to fix the faulty foundation.

Matthew 7 reminds us that whoever hears and puts into action Christ's teachings is like a wise man who builds his house upon a rock, a solid foundation. The person who builds on the Word of God is well-equipped to withstand life's storms.

The foolish man, however, takes no time to count the cost and builds anywhere he wants. His foundation is unstable—a mixture of airy philosophies and sand. In the middle of a storm, it all collapses with a crash and disappears beneath the deluge. Without a solid foundation, there is no standing strong.

If we are going to stand strong against authority abuse—if we plan to prevent it in our own lives—we must build our actions upon a solid, foundational understanding of godly authority. We won't know what is crooked unless we first know what is straight. We find our straight path, our solid foundation, when we answer this: "Where does godly authority come from?"

Where does godly authority come from?

Do you remember why Jesus so amazed the Jews? *"The crowds were amazed at his teaching, because he taught as one who had authority, and not as their teachers of the law"* (Matthew 7:28–29). The Jews were amazed because they did not know where Jesus got His authority. He spoke and acted with such obvious power—but how? What was the source of His certainty, His sureness, His assertion that He had the say-so? It puzzled them so much that even the Jewish religious leaders admitted they did not understand.

> *Jesus entered the temple courts, and, while he was teaching, the chief priests and the elders of the people came to him. "By what authority are you doing these things?" they asked. "And who gave you this authority?"*　(Matthew 21:23)

As I once heard Pastor Ray McCollum explain, we can find the answer to that question in a conversation between Jesus and a Roman centurion who, though a Gentile, was a devout and God-fearing man.

> *When Jesus had entered Capernaum, a centurion came to him, asking for help. "Lord," he said, "my servant lies at home paralyzed and in terrible suffering." Jesus said to him, "I will go and heal him." The centurion replied, "Lord, I do not deserve to have you come under my roof. But just say the word, and my servant will be healed. For I myself am a man under authority, with soldiers under me. I tell this one, 'Go,' and he goes; and that one, 'Come,' and he comes. I say to my servant, 'Do this,' and he does it."*
> (Matthew 8:5–9)

Notice that the centurion didn't say "I, too, am a man who has authority." He told Jesus, "*I myself am a man **under** authority, with soldiers under me*" (v. 9, emphasis added). He recognized that Jesus' power and authority was from the Father. Jesus had been sent by the Father and was in this sense a *delegate* for the Father. As Romans 13:1 explains, true authority is given only by God:

> *Everyone must submit himself to the governing authorities, for there is no authority except that which God has established. The authorities that exist have been established by God.*

Authority Abusers

The book of Genesis tells us that, from the start, God set some parts of His creation over others:

> Then God said, "Let us make man in our image, in our likeness, and let them rule over the fish of the sea and the birds of the air, over the livestock, over all the earth, and over all the creatures that move along the ground." (Genesis 1:27)

As Scripture records, God continued this precedent of putting some in authority over others. Man, for instance, was given authority over woman (Ephesians 5:22–23); kings and presidents authority over countrymen (2 Chronicles 9:8); and pastors authority over congregations (2 Corinthians 13:10). Because God has established these authority relationships, they ought to reflect His character. That's why, right after telling women to submit to their husbands, Paul admonished husbands to imitate Christ: *"Husbands, love your wives, just as Christ loved the church and gave himself up for her"* (Ephesians 5:25). All authority must mirror the character of its Creator.

What's It For?

Genesis 2:15 says, *"The Lord God took the man and put him in the Garden of Eden to work it and take care of it."* This is the first time God put man in authority over anything. Notice that it is one of the very first things He did with His universe; while a "new creation" smell still lingered in the air, God posted a "Man at Work" sign and stepped back. In that perfect, flawless time and place, the institution of godly authority followed God's design; it demonstrated this unshakable truth: **Godly authority, without exception, nurtures and cultivates whatever is placed under it.**

This truth applies to all kinds of authority in all kinds of relationships—in marriages, in churches, in the home, in the workplace. As my wife and I wrote in *Crazy House, Sane House*, for instance, a husband is responsible not only for caring for his wife, but also for encouraging her to grow in her strengths and giftings. Why? Because a husband has authority over his wife. And just as God intended Adam to nurture and cultivate the garden placed in his care, God expects man to encourage his wife as well. A woman should thus submit to her husband; God intends for her life to be led, fed, and nurtured by her husband into beautiful fruit.

This principle of encouragement extends to the church and business contexts, as well. If the person in authority over you has an open hand, there's nothing you won't be able to do. Like a loving father, he should be happy—even excited—to support you in whatever God calls you to do. Why? Because godly authority is selfless, desiring those under it to blossom and grow. Thus, those who exercise godly authority never feel threatened by their "children" but rather rejoice in their accomplishments.

Policemen provide an example of godly authority since they have the best interests of those under them at heart. We teach children that policemen are their friends—even though we may get uptight at the sight of police cruisers parked along the highway—and that if they are ever lost, they should ask a police officer for help. Why? Because that police officer, that person of authority, that person who's "in charge" is a guarantee to every law-abiding citizen: when you need help, you have on your side the best your government can offer. Authority is always looking out for the good of those it governs.

When authority looks out for those under it, the "ruled" respond with obedience to the guidelines intended for their good. To continue the policeman example, I usually try keeping my highway speed within five or six miles of the posted speed limit. This way I don't feel a guilty jolt of adrenaline whenever I round a corner and see a police car. Instead of stomping on the brake pedal, hoping I can slow down before the officer scans me, I simply motor on my way. In fact, seeing a police car makes me more confident because I know I don't have to worry about a crazy driver barreling down behind me at 90 mph; he would have to first get past the policeman, who would exercise his authority to keep me safe. That's godly authority with a gun! (See Romans 13:3–4.)

A pastor must care for the spiritual well-being of his congregation.

As a pastor, I understand first-hand that I have similar responsibilities. As a husband is responsible for nurturing and encouraging his wife, a pastor must lead and encourage his congregation. As a policeman cares for the well-being of citizens, a pastor must care for the spiritual well-being of his congregation.

There are vast responsibilities that accompany my office. Like all pastors I sometimes miss the mark; I have come to realize that some of our greatest successes come out of our worst failures. When we fail, though, we must be willing to admit our mistakes, learn from them, and strive for greater God-centered maturity. It's when we make excuses for ourselves that our Christian life starts stagnating—and we start abusing our authority.

In Ephesians 4, Paul outlines the various ministries in a church:

And He Himself gave some to be apostles, some prophets, some evangelists, and some pastors and teachers, for the equipping of the saints for the work of ministry, for the

edifying of the body of Christ, till we all come to the unity of the faith and of the knowledge of the Son of God, to a perfect man, to the measure of the stature of the fullness of Christ.
(vv. 11–13)

We've heard these Scriptures so many times that we almost don't hear them at all any more; they just patter away in the background like elevator music.

But what do they mean? God's Word deserves more than a passing glance; let's take a deeper look at these verses by focusing on the office of pastor.

As a shepherd tends his sheep, the job of a pastor (which literally means "shepherd") is to tend his flock, the flock the Lord has given him. Remember, when Peter said he loved the Lord, Jesus replied, "Feed my sheep." As a spiritual overseer, the pastor is to look after, teach, and empower the people in his church. According to Ephesians 4, the office of pastor was given for three specific reasons:

1. *"The perfecting of the saints."*

I believe the word *"perfecting"* here refers to sanctification. Sanctification is the work of the Holy Spirit in which our human nature is transformed, through a lifelong process encompassing the whole of man's being, into more Christlikeness. As a pastor, I have both the authority and responsibility to present God's Word to my people, an essential element in the sanctification process. I should give them a balanced understanding of what Scripture teaches—mercy and judgment, challenges and grace—and if I do my job correctly, they will be armed with scriptural truth for every situation. And if they don't know what God's Word says about a particular issue, they will know how to find out. The Holy Spirit is responsible for sanctification but occasionally chooses to accomplish it through human tools. I must let the Holy Spirit do His work and I will do mine; God will not do my job, and I cannot do His.

2. *"The work of the ministry."*

Good pastors, despite their failures, know how to effectively lead laborers into ministry work by example—meeting people's needs, correcting congregants when necessary, and leading others to Christ. I cannot expect my congregation to understand Christian service unless I model it for them. That's why, no matter what kind of outreach or function we do, chances are good that Bishop Bloomer will be there at some point, dressed up—or sleeves rolled up—for the occasion.

3. *"The edifying of the body of Christ."*

To edify someone is to build them up; this requires reliable, godly, and positive input. A pastor can't build up his congregation unless he's *involved*. Part of being in authority is being in contact with the people God has placed under your care. This takes time, energy, patience, and sacrifice. Years ago, a minister shared this story:

"A few months ago, I called an elder's meeting. We had a radio program, and it always concluded by giving people a phone number they could call if they wanted prayer. We had recently made the decision to conserve the resources of our staff by putting a dedicated answering machine on that line. So when I called this meeting and told the elders that I was going to play a recording from our prayer line, they were excited. But instead of hearing the good report they expected, they sat in stunned silence as we listened to the monotone voice of a young woman.

"'I'm committing suicide. I've been looking for a reason not to, but I decided I was going to do it tonight. I called, 'cause I thought maybe you could give me a reason not to. But now I know there's no God, so I'm going to do it. Good-bye.'"

Not every ministry can operate a prayer line like this church or supply someone full time to answer it; and not every pastor can minister full time, either—some work to support families, as I did starting out. As someone once said, though, "love" is spelled T-I-M-E. At the very least, a godly authority always has time for the people it guides and leads. I do everything possible to make my office and staff members one hundred percent approachable for my congregation. I feel that anyone who has a problem, has been hurt, or feels the need to confront me about something should have the opportunity to be heard. I cannot overstate the importance of honest communication between spiritual authorities and the people they are over. I not only told my people to talk to me whenever they needed to, but also said, "If you're so mad that you're cussing inside—do it! I need to hear it; I need to know that you are that upset." How will I help them, how can I love them, if they are afraid to be themselves in front of me?

> If you're so mad that you're cussing inside—do it! I need to hear it.

But Why?

Really, we've come back to where we started: godly authority will nurture and cultivate whatever is placed under it. But there's more to authority than that—isn't there? If authority was nothing more than taking care of people, we could have an *absence* of authority but no real *abuse* of authority. Our problems, however, come from the fact that at the core of authority, one person is required to submit his or her decision-making ability to another; in a sense, being under authority means giving up some of your rights. Why would God ask us to do that?

Well, imagine for a moment a world in which there was no authority, in which no one was required to follow rules set by anyone else. Would you feel safe driving down the road with no speed limit to keep fellow drivers in check? What if you couldn't count on anyone else to stop at red lights or stop signs? Would you be worried if your local gun store sold automatic firearms to known murderers? (And the murderers wouldn't even be felons because nobody would have the authority to say they were doing wrong!)

Eventually we would be living under rules made by other people, but not because anyone was rightfully in charge; the strong would simply force the weak into submission. As the strong fought among themselves for more control and power, anarchy would ensue. This is why civilized people have voluntarily created systems of authority (government) for themselves for centuries.

On a less universal scale, think about how a warehouse for a large business works. Imagine that there was no one in charge of the warehouse. Some of the less motivated workers would perhaps spend the bulk of their day by the coffee machine and would happily collect their paycheck for drinking coffee. Problems would arise among the more motivated workers, too. What if one guy thought the product should be organized alphabetically while someone else thought it should be organized by color? There would be no rules to follow and no one to make the rules; most of their time would be spent arguing about how things should be sorted—or working to take each other's systems apart.

It wasn't always this way. In the garden of Eden both God and man had authority that was used entirely for nurturing the things under them. In God's perfect plan, mankind did what was best because it was motivated by love for God and His creation, not because it was restrained by rules. In fact there was only one rule in the whole universe at that time, a rule God laid down to protect us: don't partake of the Tree of the Knowledge of Good and Evil. (See Genesis 2:16–17.) Knowing good from evil (in other words, knowing that evil even *exists*) makes us responsible for choosing between them; that is a burden God did not want us to have to carry.

God loved us so much, though, that He wanted pure, voluntary love back. This put God in a dilemma: to let us choose Him, He had to offer us a choice between Him and something else. The problem was, everything good was already contained in Him! The only choice He could offer us was between Himself and death. Foolishly, the race of man, in its arrogance, decided it should choose "independence" from God even though this choice meant its own death and destruction. In the moment when man chose to break that *one rule* God had established, human nature became twisted for all time.

God-given authority exists now for a simple reason—to protect us from ourselves. That's why a man has a pastor over him—to help him keep his life in line with God's Word. That's why a woman has her husband over her—to serve as executive member of their partnership. That's why children have parents over them—to raise them in fear and admonition of the Lord. Remember what the centurion

Authority Abusers

said about authority in Matthew 5? Authority is a thing delegated from above, God's protective direction that filters down a chain of people who are ultimately all accountable to Him.

Chapter Three

The Making of an Authority Abuser

Pride goes before destruction, And a haughty spirit before a fall.
—Proverbs 16:18

He was called the Morning Star, the most beautiful creature ever created. His very movements were music, and he led one-third of the heavenly host in a symphony of worship to the Almighty. He had been delegated authority second only to God's, and he shone with the very glory that radiated from the Father's throne. His name was Lucifer. You know his story: Lucifer looked at the power and brilliance that was his, and his heart lifted up with pride. He decided he would make himself equal with God—and for his rebellion, God threw him out of heaven forever.

Authority Abusers

I know what you're thinking: How could Lucifer have been so crazy? He had the universe by the tail and then ruined it all! How could a person ever get so cute and so smart that he ended up being jealous of God? Was Lucifer *drunk*, for goodness sakes? Actually, that's not a bad analogy. You see, the way I understand it, authority is like liquor—and Lucifer had more to "drink" than was good for him.

I don't believe Lucifer smooth-talked the legions of angels that became his demonic henchmen. Can't you just see what would have happened when they got kicked out of heaven if that were true? He would have been lynched! No, Lucifer had rightful, God-given authority, but he made one critical mistake: he forgot he hadn't earned the authority and splendor he was holding. When he forgot this, he began to resent the fact that he didn't get the same kind of respect God did. *After all,* he must have thought, *my glory is nearly as brilliant as His.* The liquor of authority went to his head, and he began thinking and acting in ways he would not have done had he been sober and in his right mind.

> The way I understand it, authority is like liquor.

Now, don't misunderstand: rebellion against God is always wrong, always sin, and never justifiable. If Lucifer had known what to guard himself against, though, if he had realized the intoxicating effects of authority ahead of time, perhaps he would not have fallen into the sin that destroyed him and the spirits under him.

Lucifer established a pattern followed by every abuser of authority from that time to this. For one thing, authority abuse only springs up where there is a middleman—someone between God and the person being ruled over. That doesn't narrow things down much; as we discussed in the last chapter, every parent, pastor, or employer is in their position of authority because God delegated it to them. I think it's worth mentioning, though, that abuse shows up even more frequently in *human* chains of command—say, an associate pastor between the senior pastor and congregation members. There are many reasons for this, the biggest reason being this: people in these middleman positions have been "drinking" authority for a much shorter period of time than people in senior leadership positions. Many times, they just can't quite hold their "liquor" yet.

As they start growing tipsy with their newfound authority, these abusers succumb to the most natural inclination in the world—the desire for another "drink"! Pretty soon, priorities get disorganized, and these leaders start focusing on what will advance them in the eyes of those in authority over them. This self-centered focus (pride) is exactly what led Lucifer in rebellion against God. By the time a person is this "drunk" on authority, they no longer care about the purpose for which they were given authority in the first place. As Lucifer forgot all about leading others in the worship of Jehovah, an associate pastor may stop truly caring about the ministries he's in charge of. Whether he admits it (even to himself) or not, he will start serving himself at the expense of those under him.

Let me tell you a story as an example:

Not long ago, most of our leadership team (myself included) left town for the weekend to attend an out-of-state retreat. We left the care of the church and planning for the Sunday service in the very capable hands of a young man raised up under our ministry. On Sunday, one of our young women led the worship, and this young man presented the sermon followed by a time of ministry at the altar. Everything went smoothly until he began to take a special offering at the service's end. (We were in the middle of a building project at the time and would collect a special offering for the construction project every Sunday.) This week, as the time of offering began, a number of people got up and started leaving.

Now, our congregation has never walked out on me while I was taking an offering, and I imagine that is what stung this young man's pride. The authority he had been drinking all morning went to his head, and he no longer acted the way the young man I know and love would have acted if he were sober. "Shut the doors," he told the ushers. "Everyone can stay until we've finished taking this offering."

The ushers moved to comply, but they had half a family inside the church, half already out, and a handful of people were returning from the rest room as well, so the ushers waited several minutes in an effort to sort out the flow of people before shutting the doors. My young friend started yelling from the pulpit, scolding the ushers for not shutting the doors when he told them to. "Wasn't I speaking English?" he demanded.

When I returned from my trip, a friend from a partner church called to tell me about the incident. The people who had tried to leave were visitors from his church and had gotten up because they had to pack for an early-afternoon flight. Since they weren't part of the local congregation, they hadn't thought anything of slipping out during the closing offering for the building fund.

Obviously, the way my associate minister conducted himself was an abuse of the authority I delegated to him. He did and said things I would never have done, and he did it out of self-interest. At the time, though, he had no idea he was being abusive. It sneaked up on him, like one drink too many, the one that pushed him over the edge from a warm "drinking-glow" to intoxication. In this situation, he was no better—and certainly no worse—than any other authority abuser. It's always the same road from stewardship to abuse, with the same traps and deceptions along the way.

When challenged about their dogmatic style, abusive leaders often dismiss the serious nature of their actions and give a list of reasons to justify them. Usually they describe their dictatorship as "caring so much for the people," and often they are as deceived as the people who follow them, sincerely believing they are responsible for holiness in the lives of their parishioners. Normal people are stubborn and

> "Normal people are stubborn and weak," concludes the abuser.

weak, the pastor concludes; in order for them to live a life of godliness and holiness, he figures he must rule his congregation with an iron fist of authority.

This doesn't always happen all at once. Often a pastor starts his ministry full of fire and enthusiasm, hoping to encourage his people to become the most dynamic Christians since the day of Pentecost. All too often, though, he becomes discouraged when people fail to become transformed as quickly as he would like. Slowly his sermons move more and more toward didacticism as he aims to make his people see the high calling of God. The more time passes, the less content the pastor is to wait for God to change the people. In his self-made frustration, the pastor eventually forgets all about pointing people toward God and begins feeling personally responsible for the way they live their lives. He starts holding several church services a week just to keep people in church and "out of trouble" and holds his congregation to a standard so strict that he doesn't even make his own family comply with it. In short, he becomes a tyrant.

When a man does this, when he tries to do God's job for Him, it's no surprise that he soon feels overburdened. After trying every tactic he can think of, he grows bitter when things don't change. "Not only do these people refuse to change their lives," he thinks, "but they don't even appreciate how hard I work to keep them right with God."

And the truth is, he's right! Nobody appreciates the way he abuses his authority; they resent him, even as they follow him away from God's will. This pattern holds true no matter where you find an authority abuser. The person in authority starts out wanting the best for those under him but ends up resenting those same people. Even in the case of the most malicious authority abuse ever, I believe that the abuser, in his heart of hearts, doesn't really like being abusive, because this is not who God created him to be. The abuser is trapped in the lie just as surely as a drunk man gets trapped in his confused state.

The tragic and ironic part of the whole thing is that, with his controlling grasp, the abuser sacrifices the one thing that could really help him be a catalyst for change in his followers' lives. Look at these Scriptures:

> *Then he called his twelve disciples together, and gave them power and authority over all devils, and to cure diseases.*
> (Luke 1:1)

> *Behold, I give unto you power to tread on serpents and scorpions, and over all the power of the enemy: and nothing shall by any means hurt you.* (Luke 10:19)

The Making of an Authority Abuser

But as many as received him, to them gave he power to become the sons of God, even to them that believe on his name. (John 1:12)

As these verses show, every believer has been given spiritual authority over the rulers of darkness and the ability to change history's course. This is why it is so sad when someone trades that God-granted power for ungodly possessiveness. It is because we don't realize our power that our lives plateau into a state of stagnation. The result? People going about weekly religious rituals with no anointing, naming and claiming things that God never intended them to have in the first place, misplacing priorities, and missing their God-given destiny.

What to Do? What (Not) to Do

Paul wrote this to the Philippians while in a dungeon in Rome:

Therefore, my beloved, as you have always obeyed, not as in my presence only, but now much more in my absence, work out your own salvation with fear and trembling; for it is God who works in you both to will and to do for His good pleasure. (Philippians 2:12–13)

Paul knew it was not his *presence* that would keep the Philippians walking after God but rather his *absence,* along with their ability to develop true relationships with the Father. It would be *those* relationships—the ones between God and each Philippian believer—that would provoke their wills to do God's *"good pleasure."*

If it is not in a person to do the will of God, obey His voice, and operate under His command, no amount of browbeating will save him. The only change he might

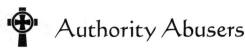

make is hiding his undisciplined behavior from the person trying to control him. That's how a person learns to fear earthly authority more than he or she fears God. Any time a man is feared more than God, idolatry is present—and God has said, *"I, the LORD your God, am a jealous God"* (Exodus 20:5). He will not share His glory, for He alone is supreme and none is to be feared except Him.

Every pastor should have this truth branded on his heart: "There is nothing I can do to whip a person into shape if he is determined to walk after the flesh." Individuals must go through their own experiences in life that will ultimately draw the defining line of who they are and which paths they will take. Those who walk after the Spirit are convicted when they are in error and seek to right the things that have gone wrong; it is the Spirit who convicts, though, not the pastor. When a person has an intimate relationship with God, his spirit becomes less accessible to outside voices that seek to steer him in the opposite direction of God's designs.

> It is the Spirit who convicts us of sin, not the pastor.

In contrast, beating on people with condemnation is a human tactic of control. It is not biblical, and even Jesus' ministry did not operate out of condemnation. *"For God sent not his Son into the world to condemn the world; but that the world through him might be saved"* (John 3:17).

I want you to picture something: imagine you are driving peaceably along when you see a police officer with a car pulled over. The driver, still inside the car, has license and registration in hand. The policeman, hat wadded up in one hand, is throwing a fit, stomping back and forth alongside the car, banging on the car roof. He's red in the face, and he's screaming at the top of his lungs.

The Making of an Authority Abuser

"You were fifteen miles an hour over the speed limit! FIFTEEN! Do you know how fast that is? You should be ashamed of yourself! How many times do I have to tell you to drive slower than the posted speed limit?! But, noooooo, you have to drive FIFTEEN MILES AN HOUR OVER! I work so hard, trying to keep these streets safe; I talk to you, I give you tickets, and I keep telling you you're going to jail if you don't change your ways! Why? Why do I have to tell you over, and over..."

Now, that little scene is a tad scary because it's definitely authority abuse. But I'll bet that you think it's more funny than scary. Why?

It's probably because all that screaming is a sure sign that the policeman feels helpless and out of control. Think about it: when most policemen approach a lawbreaker, their voices are calm, their motions unhurried. They have the power of the entire United States government behind them, and they know it. It would be completely ridiculous for them to feel personally ignored when someone breaks the speed limit because the law is much bigger than any one man. In fact, it is when police officers begin taking the actions of lawbreakers personally that we see instances of police brutality and other abuses of the legal system.

Now, apply this lesson to the rest of life. What are we forced to conclude when we find a parent screaming at her children, nagging them, belittling them? A husband criticizing his wife, finding fault with all she does? What about a pastor who paces his platform like a wild animal, practically foaming at the mouth as he rails against his congregation's "sinfulness"?

That's right. One of the biggest reasons leaders abuse their authority is that they feel out of control—like they can't do their jobs right. And, like I said before, this feeling of impotence often arises because leaders are trying to do God's job. Of course, they can't do his job because He doesn't *want* them to have that much control. Still, they neglect their true spiritual responsibilities in the effort to succeed. Then nobody's work gets done, and things ultimately collapse into a horrid jumble.

I honestly believe that if potential authority abusers would free themselves from the perceived responsibility that *they* must change peoples lives, they would never become abusive. They would have the liberty to love people—even sinners—just the way they are and help people take the "small steps," like understanding God's principles for finances. A leader like that would soon begin seeing the cumulative effect of slow, healthy growth in some of his people. The people who refuse to grow, then, would not seem like such a terrible blot on the record. The pastor would begin seeing how these things depend entirely on God.

The Even Darker Side

There is another cause of authority abuse, and it amounts to an unhealthy desire for power or influence. Often abusers of this kind have been abused themselves or come from a background in which they were not valued as people. You see, abuse breeds abuse. People who have been abused set out to "fix" themselves while unknowingly slipping into the habits and philosophies of the people who abused them. They approach life with fierce determination to be *somebody*, even though they never truly believe they are valuable.

Often, an abusive ministry is one that has either broken away from or been kicked out of an established church because this type of abuser cannot tolerate being under authority—only wielding it. The abuser's hunger to be influential demands that he have a leadership position. Sometimes he believes his humble background gives him a special perspective, as though he's "paid his dues"; sometimes he just needs to prove he's important. Regardless of the reasons, though, he feels he needs a position of authority to attract and control people who have strong talents. He then uses these people as facilitators to sustain and advance his position of authority because he doesn't trust any of his own gifts or abilities. These facilitators help the authority abuser create an atmosphere of control. Because he needs the gifts of other people, the abuser is normally terrified of losing control over others. He seeks ever-increasing authority in an awful, vicious cycle.

> The abuser is normally terrified of losing control over others.

Everyone, even the wounded and hurting, has a God-given gift or talent. It doesn't take an authority abuser long to learn that hurting people are almost pathetically eager to contribute their gifts in return for affirmation. Abusive ministries thus are often more sensitive than others to the needs and hurts of people at their services and better than average at getting people involved in the church—not because they genuinely and purely care but because they *need* the gifts these hurting people bring. Authority abusers don't have the ability to nurture and refresh the people under them the way a leader should, and, eventually, their people grow tired, get used up. When a person who is under authority abuse no longer has the emotional or spiritual energy to pour into the abuser's work, the abuser lets him or her fade into the background, as newer, freshly-grateful faces take over the work of propping up the authority figure.

Or the "used-up" individual may be given a chance to commit himself completely and irrevocably to the abuser's ministry. If the individual is willing to totally forfeit producing anything on his own (by pouring everything into the abusive ministry), the abuser begins pouring back into him, grooming him for service. Sometimes an abuser claims he is preparing this person to be sent out; the truth, though, is that nobody leaves. Often an authority abuser is surrounded by a small circle of codependent followers who live and die by his words. These facilitators are like the eunuchs Queen Jezebel surrounded herself with (2 Kings 9:32). Much more spiritual-looking than the rest of the congregation, more fervently defensive of the ministry, they have been spiritually "castrated" and can reproduce only vicariously through the ministry of the abuser.

The worst of it is that abuse almost always propagates itself. I knew a boy (now a man), for instance, whose parents both worked all day long. His father was an abusive alcoholic. Every morning, this boy was responsible for waking his siblings after his parents left for work, packing their lunches, feeding them breakfast, and sending them to school. Then he had to pack his own lunch and go to school. After school he was required to clean the house and have dinner mostly ready and waiting when his parents came home late in the evening. If he failed to have things just right, he could count on being beaten by his father.

Now how do you suppose this boy treated his siblings? The fact is, he was abusive. He wasn't as abusive as his father, but he used his authority to save his skin, to make his siblings his helpers, and, occasionally, to turn his siblings into targets for the pain and anger he couldn't vent anywhere else. The simple truth: abuse bred abuse.

Imagine a situation in which a church leader was found to be guilty of adultery. There is no doubt he would be wrong and in sin, and scriptural discipline should be administered. Suppose, though, that the discipline brought him to a place of real repentance, but that the authority over him refused to restore him to Christian fellowship as the apostle Paul instructed. (See 1 Corinthians 5:1–3, and 2 Corinthians 2:5–8.) That would be an abuse of authority, and Paul said it could cause the repentant man to *"be swallowed up with overmuch sorrow"* (v 7).

I have seen this happen and seen what results from it. I have seen men leave the churches that would not restore them and start their own ministries. They become the kind of people we talked about at the beginning of this section: distrustful of all authority but their own, surrounding themselves only with people who will help boost them toward their desires, abusing others in an effort to feel worth something.

In Sum

If you could distill the causes of authority abuse down to their most elemental level, you would find at the bottom of your beaker an old and familiar enemy: the sin of pride. Don't think I am talking about arrogance; for most authority abusers, that comes much, much later in the game. When I speak of pride, I am speaking of the simple (and, in our fallen state, very natural) inclination to think of oneself before thinking of others. Or, if you'd rather, it's our inclination to *prefer* our own interests over the interests of those around us.

Authority Abusers

There is hardly a soul that hasn't wished at one time or another that he could hold in his hands real power, if only for a moment, to set the world the way he thought it should be. Authority abuse is what happens when someone gets that power and is not reverent in the use of it. It is, in fact, the worst kind of irreverence—a disregard for the Creator's right to have His handiwork treated with honor.

Chapter Four

Recognizing Authority Abuse

It's hard to identify an abusive leader, especially if you're involved in the situation. They really are like predators in a lot of ways. They remind me of spiders. Spiders have no teeth, no way to break down food for themselves, so they spin beautiful webs to trap passing insects instead. Once a spider has caught an insect, it sucks out the bug's protein- and nutrient-rich juices, draining it until it is dead and dry.

Now, insects are incredibly strong for their size; a spider couldn't simply begin bleeding one of them to death without getting mauled—especially since spiders often victimize insects that are actually stronger and more powerful than they are. How does the spider do it? Well, every spider is equipped with a poisonous bite that is deadly to small creatures. They are also equipped with a second kind of poison, a special nerve-toxin. This toxin paralyzes the victim's ability to resist but leaves it very much alive so its life juices can be easily extracted.

It is something similar to this paralyzing toxin that makes authority abusers so hard to recognize. They are always deceitful and manipulative; no one announces, "I am abusing you right now, but you have to obey me anyway." No, they act very concerned about the welfare of the people they are using and may even use that "worry" as a lever for emotional blackmail. Their victims rarely have more than a vague sense something is not exactly "right"— and the abusers always make sure the victims conclude it's their own fault.

I know of a young lady who grew up in an abusive household. She was very bright, an excellent student, and, after high school, she went on to a very prestigious private college. It wasn't until her second year as an Education major, while she was studying child development, that she realized she had been verbally and emotionally abused her entire life. She had always thought what went on in her household was normal, because her spirit was paralyzed by the abuser's toxin.

If you need to ask yourself and God, "Am I prey for a soul-sucking, spiritual spider," I have a very simple definition of authority abuse that can help you answer that question: **Authority abuse is any situation in which an authority figure's influence eclipses that of God's or disrupts God's divine *order* of authority**. Of course what's easy to say isn't always easy to see. I think it's time we talked about the demonic spirit behind nearly every, if not all, instances of authority abuse.

Recognizing Authority Abuse

In Revelation 2:18–29, Jesus addressed a church that had this demonic spirit at work amongst its people:

> *And to the angel of the church in Thyatira write, "These things says the Son of God, who has eyes like a flame of fire, and His feet like fine brass: 'I know your works, love, service, faith, and your patience; and as for your works, the last are more than the first. Nevertheless I have a few things against you, because you allow that woman Jezebel, who calls herself a prophetess, to teach and seduce My servants to commit sexual immorality and eat things sacrificed to idols. And I gave her time to repent of her sexual immorality, and she did not repent. Indeed I will cast her into a sickbed, and those who commit adultery with her into great tribulation, unless they repent of their deeds. I will kill her children with death, and all the churches shall know that I am He who searches the minds and hearts. And I will give to each one of you according to your works. Now to you I say, and to the rest in Thyatira, as many as do not have this doctrine, who have not known the depths of Satan, as they say, I will put on you no other burden. But hold fast what you have till I come. And he who overcomes, and keeps My works until the end, to him I will give power over the nations; he shall rule them with a rod of iron; they shall be dashed to pieces like the potter's vessels'; as I also have received from My Father; and I will give him the morning star. He who has an ear, let him hear what the Spirit says to the churches."*

Jesus referred to a particular evil woman who was clearly in a place of influence as "Jezebel" because her behavior and the fruit that grew on the branches of her life was so much like the wickedness of the queen Jezebel we read about in the Old Testament. (See 1 Kings 16–21; 2 Kings 9.) It appears this woman of Thyatira was acting under the influence of the same evil spirit, or kind of spirit, as Queen Jezebel of old, and with similar results. To put it briefly, both "Jezebels" abused their authority with powerful use of deceit and manipulation. In addition to teaching idolatry, the first Jezebel was also an open murderess; and Jesus characterized the teaching of the second Jezebel as *"the depths of Satan."*

Who's Your Doorway to God?

Anyone who acts under the influence of the spirit that typified these two women invariably puts himself between God and the people under him; and I believe that a leader who stands between God and anyone else is opening himself to influence by the Jezebel spirit.

To the children they abused, the priests represented God.

As I write this, the Roman Catholic Church is weathering yet another round of bad publicity because a number of priests have been found guilty of child molestation. How were so many children manipulated and convinced to keep quiet about their horrible secrets? The answer is this: to the children they abused, these priests represented God. In the nature of the Jezebel spirit, deceit and manipulation obscured who the *real* Authority was.

The most frightening thing about the abusive behavior engendered by the Jezebel spirit is that a person who dabbles in idolatry almost always ends up swallowed by it. The commentators of the NIV Study Bible made this note about the Old Testament Jezebel and her husband, King Ahab: "The names of Ahab's sons (Ahazia, 'The LORD grasps'; Joram, 'The LORD is exalted') suggest that Ahab did not intend to replace the worship of the Lord with the worship of Baal but to worship both deities in a syncretistic way."

Recognizing Authority Abuse

In other words, when Ahab decided to make room for Jezebel's idolatry, he didn't plan on setting Baal worship between God and the children of Israel. He just wanted to tack it on, so to speak, because the power and sensuality of Jezebel appealed to him. A few short years later, though, Elijah could truthfully say, *"I alone am left a prophet of the Lord;* [who was willing to stand up and be recognized] *but Baal's prophets are four hundred and fifty men"* (1 Kings 18:22).

I am sure it was the same with the abusive Roman Catholic priests. They did not intend to lead their followers completely away from God—only to use their authority as a bit of "leverage" to get some personal satisfaction. I believe it worked better than they had intended because when an already impressionable young person goes to an adult of religious authority, it's easy for the child to be manipulated into thinking salvation and forgiveness can come only through that leader. In short, these priests replaced God in the minds of the young people they abused. They made themselves idols and consequently taught idolatry to children. Although I'm sure it was never phrased this way, the children learned that enduring abuse was an act of worship; it was their service to God, the only way they could be sure to earn the priests' favor and thus, the favor of God. Before the sexual abuse, there was an abuse of authority.

Children naturally want to please those in authority, and they are inclined to believe that those placed over them have their best interest at heart. This is also a characteristic of wounded and vulnerable adults, though. An individual driven to guilt and shame for her sins, as an example, can easily be manipulated by a leader who convinces her he holds the key to her forgiveness. Some women can attest, in fact, to being lured into ungodly relationships

53

with leaders during a state of vulnerability while seeking spiritual guidance. Instead of being pointed in the right direction—toward Christ—they were given a shoulder to cry on and a warm embrace that led to years of involvement impossible to break, no matter how hard they tried.

Anyone with a wounded heart, feelings of inferiority, or a guilty conscience can be vulnerable to a mind-set that looks to a pastor or leader for affirmation instead of to God. Abusers make a practice of fueling this fear and self-doubt with even more uncertainty so that their victims depend more and more on them. Once the authority figure has replaced God as affirmation-giver, it's not too long until he's replaced God in other areas as well. Sometimes abusers provide affirmation by placing a person with a wounded spirit and low self-esteem in a position of authority and then convincing that individual that he or she would never be a success without the leader.

Basically, an abusive leader will do anything to foster dependence on himself. For the victim, the process is something like walking down a gentle but extremely slippery hillside. The victim might not even notice she is going downhill; and even if she does, she may not be able to get back up again—every step sends her slipping further down.

The subtle process of abuse is somewhat like being anesthetized for surgery as well. A good anesthesiologist doesn't strap your mask on, turn around, and flip on a torrent of the sleeping gas. Instead she adjusts your mask, asks if you're comfortable, and continues making small talk. A lot of patients don't notice when her hand slips back to turn on a trickle of gas, and most don't remember at what point they fall asleep. Similarly, in authority abuse, the victim never sees it happening—and sometimes the authority figure doesn't either! Sadly, though, the abuse of authority is often a deliberate, selfish exercise of manipulation by a person whose own imbalanced and ungodly emotional needs demand that other people look up to him.

I once heard the story of a young man so bent on pleasing his earthly leader that he became convinced that he couldn't look at the True Master—God—and that God couldn't look at him if his human spiritual leader was not pleased. This flies directly in the face of God's Word. Remember what Jesus taught? There can be only one master:

> *No man can serve two masters: for either he will hate the one, and love the other; or else he will hold to the one, and despise the other.* (Matthew 6:24)

Jesus applied this truth to the pursuit of money, so we usually think of it in that context. It is a principle, however, that can be applied throughout all of life, and the message is clear: you cannot serve God—*the* Master—while simultaneously showing more loyalty to another master—mankind. We must be wary because leaders, both inside the church and out, often use tactics of fear, shame, and guilt to control and manipulate their followers. Remember, though, that any time man's voice is stronger than God's voice, it stunts spiritual growth, opens the door to other sins, causes division in marriages, and even destroys entire families.

Whenever a leader deceives people into thinking *he* is the only way for them to receive or hear from God, he has begun abusing his authority. That deception places him in a position that only God is supposed to occupy—and the Lord is less than pleased with that. Remember what He said in Exodus 20:5: *"For I the Lord thy God am a jealous God."* He will not share His glory; as a pastor, I would never dare to become one of the wolves, leading His sheep away by competing for His position as *the* Shepherd.

I know of an instance in which a man (I'll call him "Thomas") began seeking God about owning a home. God answered his prayers by beginning to prosper his business and by opening the door for the man to buy an affordable home for his family.

Seeing that all these things had been taken care of, one of his friends asked Thomas, "Well, what are waiting for? God has opened the door and answered your prayers. When are you going to move in?"

"Well," Thomas replied, "I need to take it to the authority first."

Realizing that Thomas's idea of authority was the pastor (not God), his friend responded, "But you've been praying, and God has answered your prayers by giving you the finances and the home to purchase. What will you do if the 'authority' tells you not to purchase a home for your family?"

"Well," Thomas answered, "I guess I'd just give that dream up, because if God is really leading me in this direction, then He will let my leader know as well."

This was truly a pastor in a position where he did not belong, verging upon self-destruction and the wrath of God. Christ died so that men and women could come directly to Him, and while we should maintain *respect* for those in authority over us, we should not use them as our *rights of passage* to hear from God. Christ alone is our High

Priest. (See Hebrews 4:14–15.) His death and resurrection have already paved the path to the Father. He even left us the road map, the Word of God, by which to get there. Nowhere does the Bible say a Christian's life should be micromanaged by the earthly spiritual authority over him. Instead it gives guidelines for living a godly life—including guidelines for taking responsibility of decisions God has given each individual. These individual decisions are not for a pastor to decide unless the Christian simply cannot understand what the Bible says on the subject; even then, it is the pastor's responsibility to lead the seeker through the Word toward the answer—not to give him commands.

Have You Been Taught to Fear Your Leader?

I vividly remember my childhood prayer—"Dear God, please don't let the pastor find out that I sinned"—and I know for a fact that my pastor wasn't the only leader to control his people with fear. This sense of fear, an indicator of abuse, is most noticeable in conservative, "old-school" ministries. Usually the minister begins with good intentions, trying to mold his parishioners into stellar Christians. Far too often, though, I've seen it degenerate to a point where the leader, showing a lack of Christ's character, uses his people's weaknesses against them. Remember, his responsibility is to nurture and protect the people God has placed in his church. Thundering self-righteous judgment from the pulpit is neither Christlike nor edifying, and controlling people through emotional blackmail is completely sinful. A pastor should be both firm and compassionate,

> It is the pastor's responsibility to lead the seeker through the Word

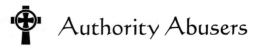

never too eager to learn about other people's faults. After all, it's not news that we all sin.

> *Again, the gift of God is not like the result of the one man's sin: The judgment followed one sin and brought condemnation, but the gift followed many trespasses and brought justification. For if, by the trespass of the one man, death reigned through that one man, how much more will those who receive God's abundant provision of grace and of the gift of righteousness reign in life through the one man, Jesus Christ.* (Romans 5:16–17 NIV)

One person (Adam) is responsible for all sin while one Person (Jesus) is responsible for all righteousness. We live with the guilt that originated in one person's disobedience. When Adam, the first representative of our race, made his decision to sin, all humanity turned away from God and our nature became bent toward evil. As Romans 5 says, though, Jesus came as the *"second Adam",* another God-chosen representative for the human race, and gave us the opportunity to turn back to God. So the Gospel is not a message of condemnation as some abusive leaders would have us think but rather a message of freedom and empowerment. We should be able to rejoice—not roll in worry, shame, guilt, and fear—because, although we received death-row sentences, the spiritual parole officer descended to the basement prison cell where we were and worked out a deal for our release.

Unfortunately, though, we in the body of Christ have become so hypocritical that if a person who sincerely loves God commits a sin that becomes publicly known, we mark the individual. We talk about him, we avoid him, we hold him up as a moral lesson. Every time a pastor is tempted to do this, he should ask himself, "What if God marked me every time I committed a sin? What if He made an example of me?"

Instead of restoring our sisters and brothers, we've sought to control them by holding them hostage in their weaknesses: "Don't forget, I know you have this problem; don't go too far and don't rub me the wrong way or I'll expose you." Spiritual blackmail is a terrible testimony for the body of Christ. When a sister or brother is overtaken by sin, we—the spiritual ones—are to restore that individual to Christ, not through name-calling and self-righteous finger-pointing, but through the love and guidance of Christ. We're to remember that although we ourselves may not be actively engaged in sinful acts at the time, we're all prone to become enticed with and engage in certain sinful activities when the opportunity presents itself. Thinking you're too spiritual to be tempted by anything is the greatest weapon Satan could ever use to ensnare you with your own deceit.

> How did God find out about your sin? You did it in front of Him!

Periodically I challenge my people: "How can you be worried about God showing your sin to me when you've already shown it to Him? How did God find out about it? You did it in front of Him—and, when you repented, He forgave you! And now you're more worried about me finding out than you are about God? If you don't have a problem with God knowing, let it all hang out! Don't you dare revere a man—especially me—more than God!" I don't want to be one of the men who exalt themselves above the power of God. So what if "Bishop" knows?! So what if your pastor knows? You should care about God knowing—and you should *want* Him to know. I want to get delivered by God; I want Him to help me with my sin!

And you know what? God is so faithful to His people that He has never showed me someone else's mess unless

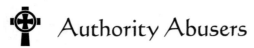

he or she was set in sinful ways to the point of desiring sin over holy living. And even then, it was only when their sin was hurting the rest of the church that God spoke to me. Otherwise, it's none of my business. I like to help my people if I can, but I refuse to take God's authority over sin into my own hands. Remember, it is *God* whom we are to fear:

> Let us hear the conclusion of the whole matter: Fear **God** and keep His commandments, for this is man's all. For God will bring every work into judgment, including every secret thing, whether good or evil.
> (Ecclesiastes 12:13–14, emphasis added)

Has Your Immediate Authority Been Overridden?

We cringe when we hear about leaders who become too involved in the day-to-day activities of marriages and families. I think usually we're just reacting under a certain "gross-out" factor; it's unpleasant for most people to think about a third person having a say in their personal lives. This kind of abuse, though, is actually more serious than gross. When a leader begins dictating policies for households that are not his own, he starts doing something the Lord never approves of: overriding the God-ordained order of authority.

> And it came to pass after these things that Naboth the Jezreelite had a vineyard which was in Jezreel, next to the palace of Ahab king of Samaria. So Ahab spoke to Naboth, saying, "Give me your vineyard, that I may have it for a vegetable garden, because it is near, next to my house; and for it I will give you a vineyard better than it. Or, if it seems good to you, I will give you its worth in money." But Naboth said to Ahab, "The LORD forbid that I should give the inheritance of my fathers to you!" So Ahab went

into his house sullen and displeased because of the word which Naboth the Jezreelite had spoken to him; for he had said, "I will not give you the inheritance of my fathers." And he lay down on his bed, and turned away his face, and would eat no food. But Jezebel his wife came to him, and said to him, "Why is your spirit so sullen that you eat no food?" He said to her, "Because I spoke to Naboth the Jezreelite, and said to him, 'Give me your vineyard for money; or else, if it pleases you, I will give you another vineyard for it.' And he answered, 'I will not give you my vineyard.'" Then Jezebel his wife said to him, "You now exercise authority over Israel! Arise, eat food, and let your heart be cheerful; I will give you the vineyard of Naboth the Jezreelite." (1 Kings 21:1-7)

Now remember when God first gave the land of Canaan to the Israelites, He told them, *"The land must not be sold permanently, because the land is mine and you are but aliens and my tenants. Throughout the country that you hold as a possession, you must provide for the redemption of the land"* (Leviticus 25:23). First Kings isn't clear about whether or not Ahab intended to buy the vineyard permanently and thus break the law God had established; even if Ahab was willing to obey the law, though, Naboth had the right to turn him down. Being steward of a family heritage was a serious thing, and the decision to accept or reject Ahab's offer was given to Naboth by the Lord Himself. So, despite the fact that Ahab had offered a very fair bargain, Naboth was not unreasonable in holding onto his vineyard—only conservative.

Ahab recognized the rightness of Naboth's decision, and while his actions—sulking like a spoiled child—were not godly, his thinking certainly was: he accepted the fact that God had given Naboth immediate authority over the vineyard even though he himself had authority over Naboth. Jezebel, however, recognized no such thing. She said to Ahab, in effect, "Some king you are! Stop being such a baby! I'll get the vineyard if you don't have the stomach for it."

She arranged to have Naboth murdered and then gave the ownerless vineyard to Ahab. It seemed legitimate because there was a kangaroo-court trial before Naboth was "executed," and it was also perfectly legal for a king to take over stewardship of land if the immediate owner passed away. But God was not fooled, and He sent the prophet Elijah to tell Ahab, *"Because you have sold yourself to do evil in the sight of the* LORD: *Behold, I will bring calamity on you"* (1 Kings 21:20). Notice that the judgment didn't come just because Ahab agreed to murder; it was because, under the influence of the Jezebel spirit, Ahab *"sold* [himself] *to do evil."* That evil was overriding and warping the structure of authority God had set in place, and for this there would be punishment.

> Jesus Himself never violated God's order of human authority.

You see, the order of authority means so much to God that Jesus Himself never violated it. As a child, Jesus submitted to His parents even when they didn't understand who He was or what He meant when He explained His calling. (See Luke 2:41–51.) In fact, the first time he was recognized as the Lamb of God, Jesus was *submitting* Himself to the work of God accomplished by the baptism ministry of John.

When Jesus came to the river Jordan to be baptized, John didn't want to do it. He said, in effect, "I can't baptize you! This doesn't make any sense. I need you to baptize me!"

John had a point, too; he was "only" a great prophet while Jesus was the very Son of God! But Jesus insisted. After all, how could God be righteous if He wouldn't play by His own rules? The Father was using John to call people to repentance and commitment. It was impossible that the Son be too proud to participate. Jesus, as a leader, followed the chain of authority God had established for that point in time.

Now imagine what it would have been like if Jesus had shown up at the Jordan, tossed His robe aside, and called out, "Okay, I'm here! I'm the real authority. God sent me straight from heaven. John's been baptizing you in the water of repentance, but I am the living water. Form a line; I'll get you really straightened out. Hey, John! Come on over. You can be first. I love you—you know you've done a great job, so don't be prideful now! God will bless you if you submit to His authority, you know."

This is what happens when leaders try to run households that are not their own. They trample the God-given ministries of husbands and fathers just as surely as Jesus would have been trampling John's baptism ministry. When abusive leaders disrupt the natural flow of growth and maturity in households, they cause stable homes to collapse and already weak families to crumble. Troubled homes are easy meat for authority abusers.

Even in cases in which the home appears stable, though, the abuser may try to step in, usually subduing the man of the house first because it's impossible to really control a household without the man's cooperation. Sometimes the leader will convince the man to give up control under the guise of "supporting the leadership." Other times he will simply undermine the man by cultivating influential relationships with the wife and children until the man becomes a stranger in his own home. Regardless of how it happens, it's not "tough love"; it's manipulation, a trademark of the Jezebel spirit, plain and simple.

Anyone Can Check In.
Nobody Checks Out.

I remember preaching a three-night revival at a church where, on the surface, everything looked wonderful. I had great respect for the pastor and his wife, the praise and worship was wonderful, and the church was very clean. The building could seat about fifteen hundred people, but I noticed on the first night that only about 150 people had attended the service; I wondered why.

By the second night I had noticed the pastor's wife had a very controlling attitude. A large number of the congregation did not like her, but they fell under her authority. That same night, I was invited to their house for dinner and saw several people from the church serving the dinner. They were not working as waiters and waitresses, but in the form of household servants. They were spoken to harshly, belittled, and chastised for not giving their "services" to the "man and woman of God" for free. They were constantly told that this was "why they were cursed."

I had noticed that these people did not have a car but were using the church van to get around. They were living in the pastor's guest house, cleaning the church and the pastor's house, and meeting all the needs of the ministry. They were wholeheartedly giving their lives to the ministry, and their only compensation were the few groceries the pastor and his wife would purchase for them and their living quarters in the guest house.

Recognizing Authority Abuse

By the third night I couldn't take it anymore, so I spoke to the pastor and his wife about their treatment of the people. They explained to me that these people had been "sent to them by God" because they were such "lowlifes" and that God was using the ministry to bring them up to a level where they could be accepted by society. When I asked, "Don't you think they should be compensated on an individual basis, taught how to own a car and home, and become educated and empowered to move forth?" the pastor said the Lord had spoken to him that giving money to this type of people would hurt them. He said, "They'd never be able to excel; that's why God sent these particular people to our ministry."

This ministry had taken an obvious turn toward cultic behavior. Throughout the three nights I was there, several people in the congregation whispered to me and asked if they could come to North Carolina to sit under our ministry at Bethel Family Worship Center. They also told me, though, that they were afraid because they had been told they'd be cursed if they ever left the church or the ministry. Ultimately they remained where they were because they did not want to be cursed.

The church is in a terrible state when the saints of God are more afraid to leave mankind than they are to leave God. Today people remain in churches for years—drying up, receiving no refreshment through quenching from the Word of God, because the teaching of "obedience" has been perverted and shoved down their throats to the point where idolatry becomes an acceptable practice. All in the name of Lord!

You see, to be led by the Spirit, you must spend time in God's Word; sadly, though, the average Christian only reads the Word of God when he or she comes to church. Therefore, anything can be preached and people will believe it because they don't read the Word of God for themselves. As in the case above, for instance, many times people are told the lie that leaving a church will lead to them being cursed. You don't get cursed by leaving churches; leaving *God*, however, is a curse in itself. You cannot properly serve God while simultaneously doubting His Word and remaining in a situation that is not His will.

Only the grace of God can keep us, and it's this grace that should guide us in our actions. You simply can't live under the condemnation of "If you leave this church, you're gonna be cursed." That is blatant, ugly authority abuse.

You see, the only person on this earth who can curse you is *you*! I couldn't curse my people even if I wanted to (and I certainly don't!). A "curse" doesn't have any power unless people belive the lies and accept whatever wicked things are spoken. In other words, even if I were to speak evil over someone, I would just be making noise, *unless the listener received and believed the words I said.*

No pastor can curse you, no matter how much you "dishonor" him!

No pastor can curse you, no matter how much you "dishonor" his authority. You are the only one who can curse yourself, and this is based all on how you think. It's your thinking that will curse you, and your thinking that will block you. It's you. You're the reason why you're "cursed." It's not a demon or somebody else; it's you. The worst curse that could happen is for you to be ignorant of who God wants you to be, for you to accept lies from a leader and thus stay in a situation that is not God's will.

This curse mentality—the notion that things are going wrong in one's life because of "disobedience"—can be debilitating. If only we could break past this in the body of Christ, we could get great victory for everybody. I learned a long time ago that it doesn't matter if you tell me, "You're just no good." You see, that's only your opinion; I'm living under grace, and, through Christ, I'm just fine.

I've heard people say things like, "The reason I can't meet my bills and stuff like that is because I'm cursed." You know what I found out about the people who can't meet their bills? Do you know what the real curse is? Believe it or not, it's not the fact that they don't tithe. A whole lot of people fail to tithe, and their bills are still paid! Don't get me wrong; I believe tithing is a scriptural way to give God our best. But do you know what the real curse is? It's a refusal to sit down, look at your expenses, and make a budget that you can commit to. If you make a specific, honest plan for how you need to spend your money, I guarantee you'll find that you have a bit more than you actually need! I know that sounds complicated (more complicated than it really is), and people often don't think they could stick to a budget. So instead of trying, they shrug their shoulders and say, "Well, maybe I'm cursed."

No, you're not cursed. You need to get your eyes off of other people, what other people have, and what other people are doing.

"Well, everybody's getting a new car except for me, and I just feel so cursed."

If your car works, drive it! And remember, you don't know about your neighbor's problems with that new car, all the credit bills and overdue payments he has to deal with.

Authority Abusers

Obey the rule Grandma used at dessert time: "Don't you look on nobody else's plate."

Don't allow yourself to follow someone else and mess up what God has going for you. True grace is recognizing and appreciating what you have in your hands instead of trying to keep up with everybody else's "prosperity." No pastor can take grace and contentment away from you, even if you leave his church, for these gifts are grounded in a relationship with Jesus Christ. If you keep God first and don't allow another authority figure into that place, you can never be cursed.

Here's one last thought about any authority figure who claims to be a servant of God but threatens people with curses:

With the tongue we praise our Lord and Father, and with it we curse men, who have been made in God's likeness. Out of the same mouth come praise and cursing. My brothers, this should not be. Can both fresh water and salt water flow from the same spring? My brothers, can a fig tree bear olives, or a grapevine bear figs? Neither can a salt spring produce fresh water. Who is wise and understanding among you? Let him show it by his good life, by deeds done in the humility that comes from wisdom. (James 3:9–13)

Can You Disagree with the Leadership?

As the previous section showed, going against a person in authority who harbors a Jezebel spirit can be a terrible thing. Consider Naboth; Ahab had him killed. An abusive leader can force you out of your place in the ministry, business, or home; ruin your good name; or (less obviously) destroy your confidence in who God wants you to be.

Recognizing Authority Abuse

I have known people and situations where the abused parties were afraid to confront the abuser about his actions because "questioning the man of God" released a torrent of correction designed to pound them back into line. People have been suspended from worship teams, banned from prayer meetings, and set down for hours-long "talks" with leaders who spend the whole time discussing the supposed attitude of the person who dares question his leaders.

A young man named Jacob went to his senior pastor about some fairly serious issues. Because Jacob was the youth pastor, he was responsible for raising money that the youth group used to make trips and do activities. Jacob had a knack for raising funds, and the youth could bring in more money with a fund-raiser than the senior pastor got in a typical Sunday morning missions offering. About a year before their "talk," the pastor asked if the youth would consider donating some of the proceeds from their fund raiser to boost the church's missionary giving—a favorite project of the senior pastor's. Jacob presented the request to the youth group, and the teens decided to sacrifice one of their scheduled trips in order to help the missions program.

A few months later the pastor again asked for help, but this time told Jacob to *announce* the decision to the youth instead of making a request. The kids weren't to be consulted, he said, about how the ministry should be run; they should learn to submit to the authorities in the church, instead. As time went on, things progressed to the point where no one but the senior pastor knew what the total income from youth fund-raisers was, because no one was allowed to touch the money before he had taken out the portion allocated for missions. The money left for the youth program was hardly sufficient to keep it afloat, and Jacob faced criticism from church members for not doing enough with the teens. The kids stopped coming out for fund raisers, too, because they knew they weren't going to see the fruit of their labor.

Jacob tried to explain this to his senior pastor, who leaned back in his chair, stared at the ceiling, and drummed with his fingers as Jacob poured out his heart. As soon as Jacob finished, the pastor leaned forward in his chair, pointed his finger, and said sternly, "Well, what's clear to me is that we have some attitude issues to discuss."

This was a classic case of authority abuse. Jacob's pastor refused to take responsibility for his actions and wouldn't let anyone question his decisions. In an effort to bring Jacob back into docile submission again, the senior pastor "apologized" at the end of his rebuke. "Now, I want you to know that I'm really sorry that you've felt this way about things. I understand why you might have taken things this way, and I'm sorry. You know that I want what's best for you and the kids, and you just need to trust me, okay?"

Sadly, Jacob stayed under this abusive influence for another year and a half while the youth group dwindled down to a handful of cynical teens whose parents insisted they attend. It was then that the church board learned the pastor had stooped to actually embezzling church funds for his personal use. He was asked to resign, and Jacob also left in search of a fresh start.

The Diagnosis

These guidelines should be used carefully when you are trying to determine whether or not you are in an abusive situation. Remember, the Jezebel spirit is deceptive, and the abuse of authority can be subtle. Also remember, though, that your own perceptions can be clouded by frustration or disappointment. If you are afraid to approach your pastor about an offense, seek God about why. Is it because you are naturally shy? Because you're not sure that you're right? Or do you fear retribution of some kind?

That's just an example of how you must examine your heart; the issue goes deep and is not simple. I trust, though, that these guidelines will enable you to see the Jezebel spirit wherever it is at work. When you find it, consecrate yourself to God and let Him lead you into restoration. Later we will talk in much greater depth about restoration. First, though, I want to examine the most common kinds of authority abuse.

PART II

Dealing with Authority Abuse

Chapter Five

Pastoral Parasites

Did I commit sin in humbling myself that you might be exalted,
because I preached the gospel of God to you free of charge?
—2 Corinthians 11:7

A church in North Carolina began as a powerful ministry for developing and preparing ministers. They moved into a small area and, within about two years, they'd grown from approximately thirty members to about 150. It wasn't long before they were able to move from their first building into a much nicer one, and they just kept growing from there. God blessed them abundantly, to the point where they began equating material things with His favor on their lives. Soon they began swaying toward a "Naming and Claiming It," "Get Rich Quick," and "Everyone Should Be a Millionaire" mentality. Over time, the daily diet of that ministry became "prosperity gospel."

Around the fourth or fifth year of the ministry, the prosperity teachings grew into badgering the congregation for not attending every service and for having sinners as friends. The leaders began teaching a practice of "cutting off" family members who did not go to their church and even went so far as to reprimand families for going on vacations and celebrating holidays (Christmas and Easter included), insisting that families instead bring money spent on those occasions to the church.

Eventually, marriages inside the church began to decay. The ministry's total focus had become television and bull-horn-preaching, and there was no spiritual food for families. These family breakdowns marked the passing of the last spiritual breath in that church. The appearance of life continued, but no healthy fruit could grow on the ministry's "branches" of abuse.

It may not be obvious at first, but a lot of today's teachings on prosperity and blessing have taken on a strong flavor of the Jezebel spirit. One thing you will notice if you read the accounts of Jezebel in 1 and 2 Kings and Revelation: she is always self-serving. She pumped a lot of money and effort into the worship of Baal—but only because she believed it would increase her favor with the gods. She spent money and manipulated the government to increase her husband Ahab's power base—but only because it increased her own power at the same time.

In the same way, I believe you won't find a man preaching prosperity gospel unless it enhances his life in some way. For some, it is simply the adoration they get from congregations that love hearing about God's "fail-proof plan to prosper you." For others, it is the prestige of leading a wealthy-looking church. And for still others, it's God's money slipping into their own pockets, put there by a carefully arranged kick-back system.

No matter what their motivation, the gist of these messages are the same: that we should look prosperous and act prosperous even though our income may not permit us to carry out a lifestyle of prosperity. You might be surprised at the popularity of this ungodly teaching that everyone in the body of Christ should be a millionaire. Oftentimes, this kind of teaching implies that those who do not have wealth are somehow sinning against God! What a tragic lie.

No wonder many in the body of Christ have confused the word "prosperity" with "debt." I've received many letters through the years from people complaining of how they practiced the prosperity principles taught to them only to find their homes now suffering from overwhelming debt accumulated in order to become "prosperous."

> Many Christians have confused the word "prosperity" with "debt."

I define *prosperity debt* as spending beyond your means to present an illusion of a prosperous life that does not exist. Webster's Collegiate Dictionary defines *prosperity* as "the condition of being successful or thriving; economic well-being". How then can an individual thrive or enjoy the benefits of economic well-being if he or she, drowning in debt, pursues an image that doesn't exist? This evil teaching has caused the body of Christ to believe that the "just shall live by debt" instead of by faith. Many invest money in fine clothes, for instance, successfully looking the part but always lacking bare necessities, such as furniture and food, as they are consumed with bills.

It's tragic when a spiritual authority saddles people with this prosperity lie instead of teaching them about true riches and helping them escape a worldly value system.

Authority Abusers

There are actually churches all over America who refuse to allow people to pass their New Members classes unless they make at least $25,000 to $30,000 per year. Their theory is that allowing poorer people into the church will offset the general prosperity and diminish the "blessing of God." In many churches, if you're not part of the elite group who make astronomical sums of money, you're shunned or ostracized. Of course, this behavior contradicts what the apostle James taught about wealth:

> *My brothers, as believers in our glorious Lord Jesus Christ, don't show favoritism. Suppose a man comes into your meeting wearing a gold ring and fine clothes, and a poor man in shabby clothes also comes in. If you show special attention to the man wearing fine clothes and say, "Here's a good seat for you," but say to the poor man, "You stand there" or "Sit on the floor by my feet," have you not discriminated among yourselves and become judges with evil thoughts? Listen, my dear brothers: has not God chosen those who are poor in the eyes of the world to be rich in faith and to inherit the kingdom he promised those who love him? But you have insulted the poor…If you really keep the royal law found in Scripture, "Love your neighbor as yourself," you are doing right. But if you show favoritism, you sin.* (James 2:1–9)

People who work two or three jobs and are unable to devote time to God because they have become engulfed with debt or the pursuit of cash are running after another god, whose name is mammon (money). *"Ye cannot serve God and mammon"* (Matthew 6:24). Pastors who teach people to focus their lives on pursuing wealth are teaching worship of a false God.

You must understand that it is the will of God that all His children be blessed and in health. God truly is concerned about prospering both our soul and our economics. It is the will of God that we all pay our taxes, enjoy a vacation, and have savings. But these things are supposed to be small parts of a God-centered life; the notion that they should be central or the idea that God's plan requires outright wealth is a perversion of truth and a clear instance of authority abuse. How does it benefit someone to look prosperous but lack the means to ever enjoy *authentic* prosperity?

Breaking Out of Prosperity Debt

A mind-set of prosperity debt is really poverty mentality in disguise. You see, poverty is a way of thinking, and until your mentality changes, your lifestyle won't either. Unless you confront the lie of prosperity debt, it will eventually wipe you out.

Most of us have enough money to meet our needs but lack the discipline to manage funds properly. The Word of the Lord says that if you're faithful over a few things, He'll make you ruler over many. So why would He place you in a 17-bedroom mansion, when you can't pay $500 per month in rent? (I've spoken with people whose monthly rent was $12 per month because they were on the government-funded program called Section Eight—and yet their rent was still delinquent by several months.) If you cannot properly manage $300, then a million dollars is never going to come your way.

To break out of the poverty mind-set, first make a budget for yourself. Having this kind of commitment will help you resist the pressure to spend money you don't have. List your income and expenditures; if your expenditures exceed your income, start immediate spending cuts. Make sacrifices and eliminate those things you do not absolutely need—things like dining out, cable television, recreational shopping, going to the movies. Cook dinner at home, borrow a movie from a friend, read a book. Cook a large, simple dinner at the beginning and middle of each week and become fond of leftovers until your income is more than your expenditures.

It's important also that you find out what your real needs are. Do you really *need* another sweater—or golf club, or television—or do you merely *want* one? God will supply all your *needs* according to His riches in glory (Philippians 4:19).

Calling our wants "needs" is a spiritually dangerous practice.

Unfortunately, though, people have been taught to lie about God when it comes to obtaining things that make them feel good. They say God told them to purchase this or that, even when their purchases cause them to plummet into the abyss of debt. Converting our *wants* into *needs* like this is a spiritually dangerous practice.

Think before you buy. I once saw a pair of patent leather shoes in Chicago that I knew my wife would like, so I bought them. When I went to New York, I saw the same shoes and bought them again, not realizing I'd already purchased them in Chicago. At home I found yet another pair of the same shoes already in my wife's closet. I'd bought the same pair of shoes on three separate occasions! This could have been avoided if I had thought through each purchase instead of buying the shoes on an impulse. This time, failing to count the cost made a funny story to tell on myself, but a *lifestyle* of compulsive buying steals food from the table to buy grown-ups' toys and trades necessities for trinkets.

Many people have made serious mistakes because they were greedy and didn't know how to be satisfied and content. You must unlearn the prosperity debt lie—a downward spiral of materialism and debt is not the best God has for you! He wants more for you than living one paycheck away from being homeless. No one who tells you otherwise truly cares for your well-being.

The Word of God does not say that we can't be wealthy or have cash; it only says we cannot serve cash or allow the pursuit of money to become a priority over serving God. A story in Matthew 26 teaches an important lesson on this: the Lord is always to take precedent over money in our lives.

In this story, a woman, a prostitute by trade, approached Jesus with an alabaster jar of spikenard. Spikenard was a very, very valuable spice, usually mixed with the purest olive oil. Since investing in a business was unheard of in those days, people put their savings into valuable things that could be stored safely, like gems and precious metals. People who could not afford jewelry often invested in spices, especially spikenard.

So when this woman unexpectedly broke open the jar and poured it over Jesus' head, she was probably emptying her life's savings. She gave Him the only thing of value that she'd salvaged from her sordid lifestyle; in a sense, she offered her whole life to Him in that one act.

The disciples didn't see it this way, though. They were offended and indignant! *"To what purpose is this waste?"* they demanded (Matthew 26:8). She could have sold the spice and given the profit to the poor, they argued. It was Judas, the group's treasurer, who was most upset. As he watched the oil soak into Jesus' robe and puddle in the dust, no doubt he envisioned all that money evaporating into thin air. The disciples placed their love for mammon above the love the woman had for Jesus—but she refused to hold material possessions as more sacred than God.

> *But when Jesus was aware of it, He said to them, "Why do you trouble the woman? For she has done a good work for Me. For you have the poor with you always, but Me you do not have always."* (Matthew 26:10–11)

"Sowing" into Abuse

Some pastors continually preach prosperity and become prosperous, while the majority of their congregation remains impoverished. I want to say up front: when an authority figure demands constant giving without giving anything back to those under him, that is abuse. Any time you hear a gospel that works for only a select few, you should be suspicious, because God is no respecter of persons. The truth is, those pastors usually get rich not because they get up every morning to go to work but because they're taking what the congregation gives them.

Such leaders use God as bait in their con-artist scams by saying, "Do this for me free of charge; allow the Lord to use you." They teach that the way to become prosperous is to give, give, give—and they never teach principles of responsibility, saving, and godly discipline. There are some churches in which the pastor is so greedy that he continually pressures and badgers the congregation to give more—while he continues to take and use more for himself, pastoring from a store-front church with his fine car parked outside the door.

I pastored my church at Bethel Family Worship Center for five years without a salary, but my family was always taken care, our needs were always met. Why? Because we did not depend upon the congregation to meet our daily needs. I owned businesses and gave out of my own pocket to build and renovate a house for God first. My only goal was and still is to minister the Word of God and teach people to give of their time, talent, and finances cheerfully while bettering their own lives in the process. This is not to say I am against pastors receiving a salary; on the contrary I think they should be compensated for their services. But in obeying the principles the Lord showed me by building Him a house first, my businesses have flourished and the church has grown at an amazing rate.

We're taught to sow our bread and eat our seed.

The Bible says you reap what you sow. Those who sow into their hairdressers have wonderful hair and nothing else. Those who sow into their wardrobe have wonderful clothes but could drown in credit card bills. Those who sow into an abusive authority will reap nothing but spiritual abuse.

> *The rain comes down, and the snow from heaven, and do not return there, but water the earth, and make it bring forth and bud, that it may give seed to the sower and bread to the eater.* (Isaiah 55:10)

Too many Christians have been caught in the trap of spiritual gambling. They believe that if they give all they have, God will return the "favor" with abundance. As if Jesus was a pair of dice, the saints of God have been taught to take a throw, cross their fingers, and chant, "Come on Jesus!" while waiting for a return. We're told to "live by faith" while simultaneously being taught to sow our bread and to eat our seed. This is a huge trap.

Authority Abusers

For instance, your rent or mortgage, utility bill, car note, child-care costs, grocery bill, and other household expenses are your "breads." Tithe, offerings of thanksgiving, special pledges, charitable giving, and random acts of kindness are your "seeds." Teaching people to give all that they have is not biblical. When God gives you money, He expects you to do a number of things with it, and believe it or not, any person who gives all of his or her money to the church is outside of the will of God. Some of our money is to be reserved for "bread"; taking care of our own needs is part of God's will.

"As the rain gives seed to the sower" means seed is given for us to plant in the ministry; likewise, *"bread to the eater"* means the remainder of our income is to be disbursed within the home to meet our daily needs. Some people give money to the church that should be allotted for bills and upkeep of the home, which is why the money they give never yields a harvest. You do not have to give your rent money to the church to receive a blessing from God. You must never sow bread in the hope of reaping a tree that brings forth fruit; for only seed can do that. When you offer your bread up to God instead of your seed, God is not pleased with your sacrifice. An authority who tells you otherwise is abusive—plain and simple.

Today, I'm very careful about where I sow seeds. Some people have determined in their heart never to change; to sow into them or their ministries will only further their stubborn will, their aggression against others.

Give not that which is holy unto the dogs, neither cast ye your pearls before swine, lest they trample them under their feet, and turn again and rend you. (Matthew 7:6)

Pastoral Parasites ☩

Do not cast your pearls to swine and do not feed the children's bread to dogs. Those who are selfish do not know how to cherish spiritual gifts—which is why they pressure men to give to them rather than seeking God first in times of crisis. Those who are givers, however, know how to get God's attention in the midst of crises.

> *In those days Hezekiah was sick and near death. And Isaiah the prophet, the son of Amoz, went to him and said to him, "Thus says the LORD: 'Set your house in order, for you shall die, and not live.'" Then he turned his face toward the wall, and prayed to the LORD, saying, "Remember now, O LORD, I pray, how I have walked before You in truth and with a loyal heart, and have done what was good in Your sight." And Hezekiah wept bitterly. And it happened, before Isaiah had gone out into the middle court, that the word of the LORD came to him, saying, "Return and tell Hezekiah the leader of My people, 'Thus says the LORD, the God of David your father: "I have heard your prayer, I have seen your tears; surely I will heal you. On the third day you shall go up to the house of the LORD. And I will add to your days fifteen years.*   (2 Kings 20:1–6)

King Hezekiah was sentenced to death by God; but since he had obeyed the Lord's commands, he could turn his face to the wall and put God in remembrance of His Word: *"O Lord, remember now how I have walked before thee in truth and with a perfect heart, and have done that which is good in thy sight. "*God responded by reversing the verdict: *"I have heard thy prayer, I have seen thy tears: behold, I will heal thee."* Those who give of themselves with a pure heart and with the purest intentions know how to get God's attention. Because they give willingly and out of a cheerful heart, God opens up the windows of heaven and pours out for them innumerable overflowing blessings.

Authority Abusers

After the guest speaker had finished speaking one night during our annual tent revival, people started lining up to give their offerings to the Lord. Sensing some were giving out of an emotional response and not because God had spoken to them, I approached them. "Is this your last?" I asked each one. To those who replied, "Yes," I instructed them to put their money back in their pockets, have a seat, and enjoy the rest of the service.

Some sacrifices are necessary and biblically correct, but timing will always reveal God's will when such sacrifices are necessary. Deuteronomy 15:11 says, *"For the poor will never cease from the land; therefore I command you, saying, 'You shall open your hand wide to your brother, to your poor and your needy, in your land.'* The principle behind this verse is why many rich, successful people—even those who don't know God—give to charities; they understand the law of reciprocity.

When you do sow seed, make sure your motives are pure. You should not sow solely to receive. Instead, sowing must be an issue of the heart—full of compassion, ready to deal alms to the poor, and out of your lack into the life of one whose needs are greater than yours. Ask yourself, "Whom have I done something nice for lately without expecting anything in return?" When we obey God's principles for giving seed, He promises to bless us according to our need. As a result, we become better equipped to be blessings for others. God wants to bless us in such a way that we can be released corporately to touch each other's lives.

So the bottom line is, give according to what the Lord has blessed you with and give as He has commanded you to give. If you're a teacher, teach for the Lord; if you're a painter, paint a room in someone's house for free; if your closet is filled with shoes, find someone whose shoes are falling apart and bless them with your best pair.

It is every Christian's responsibility to learn how to handle money and gain respect for it. Tell yourself you are the head and not the tail, then take the necessary steps to make that statement true: spend wisely, give God what belongs to Him, help meet the needs of others, and take care of your own household. *"For wisdom is a defense as money is a defense"* (Ecclesiastes 7:12). If you want to feel a sense of security, refuse to bow to an abusive authority. Turn to God, exercise godly wisdom, and save some of your income. Tell yourself this is the year that you will make drastic changes in your economy; break free from the bondage of materialism. And *"if the Son makes you free, you shall be free indeed"* (John 8:36).

Chapter Six

Religious Home-Wreckers

Beware of false prophets, who come to you in sheep's clothing,
but inwardly they are ravenous wolves.
—Matthew 7:15

Kathy and David were like many American couples. She attended church regularly while he preferred going only occasionally; he never prevented his wife from pursuing her spiritual growth, though. Kathy, in her enthusiasm over finding a new church, eventually convinced David to come along one Sunday. He immediately noticed major caution signs that warranted his concern, but his wife and children had already fallen under the spell of the pastor's manipulation. They were so totally engrossed in this church that David felt helpless to deliver them out of it. He watched as his wife began running the household as if he was only her roommate, consulting him on nothing but instead seeking all her guidance and influence from the church pastor.

"Why is this man my wife's security?" David wanted to know. "And what is my position in the home now that this other man has become the strongest voice of influence over my family?"

In his effort to avoid fanning the flames of disagreement and to keep peace with his wife and children, David began compromising the structure of his own home for what the leader felt was best for his family. While the pastor increasingly became leader of their home, David became increasingly helpless and hopeless as his voice was silenced, his power paralyzed. The defining point of this collapse came during a birthday celebration for his daughter, Allison.

Allison had always been a daring and ambitious teenager, and for her sixteenth birthday David's daughter decided she would like to celebrate by bungee jumping from a tall pinnacle. David adamantly refused to allow this and made it clear to his daughter and the entire family that until Allison became an adult—mature enough to make her own decisions—he would in no way support or allow such a dangerous stunt.

To David's surprise, however, the pastor made an announcement in front of Allison and all her peers that he had purchased a bungee cord and secured the area for her to take her birthday "leap of faith," despite the disapproval of Allison's father. Neither the pastor or David's wife had shared this information with David before the announcement because they knew that David strongly opposed and would not allow it. Now the secret was out.

Religious Home-Wreckers

Allison was overwhelmed with enthusiasm, and David sat on the sideline, watching helplessly as his family slipped away from him and into the hands of the man who'd taken up spiritual residence in his house without his permission.

David was forced to watch his teenage daughter climb to a high pinnacle, then plunge headfirst toward the earth. Fortunately the jump was a success and Allison was fine; but her enthusiasm at having succeeded in what her father had feared only strengthened the bond between the children, David's wife, and the pastor. All David could do was retreat into himself and wonder, "How did this happen to my family?"

For an abusive pastor or leader to move into a home there must be room for him. Unfortunately, this pastor had all the room he could possibly have wanted. Although he meant no harm, David did leave a spiritual vacuum in his home. By failing to make his own relationship with God a priority, he forfeited the spiritual authority God wanted him to exercise in his home. Even though his wife and children were visibly interested in growing after God, David was not; and his attitude of, "You go ahead if you want to," left his family looking for someone else to follow. They found that leader in the abusive pastor—and you already know the rest of the story.

"How did this happen to my family?"

Who Is My Husband?

Ron was an overachiever. He wasn't especially talented or any smarter than the average guy—he'd tell you that right off. But he was determined; he'd been taught all his life that doing things right and working hard were all he

91

needed to be a success. He never stepped on somebody else. In fact, sometimes he'd help co-workers up a rung on the ladder of success and then double his own efforts in order to pass them again. He tithed ten percent of his income, attended church twice a week, and gave five percent of every other paycheck to missions. He worked ten to fifteen hours of overtime each week and spent his Saturdays fixing up the house, keeping the lawn nice for his wife, Nina, and coaching Little League baseball. Every morning before he left for work, he and Nina would read a Psalm and pray together. Friday night was "date night," and Ron never had his cell phone along for it. To top it off, he visited a stress-management specialist once a month, to make sure that he wasn't developing any self-destructive habits.

There was only one problem. "I feel like I'm Ron's second job," Nina wrote in her journal. "I know he loves me—at least, I'm pretty sure he does. But he never asks me how I'm doing or compliments me unless we're scheduled to have time together. I can count on him to take good care of me, but I'm only one part of his life; I don't think he really wants to share the whole thing with me. I feel like I don't really know who he is. I don't know the same man that his coworkers see or that his Little-League kids know. They tell me he's wonderful, and the man I see is wonderful, but it's not the same person. Why won't he let me in close?"

Nina worked part-time at the church because they had agreed not to have children for the first seven years of marriage, and it gave her a healthy way to use her strong organizational and interpersonal skills. She was good at her job, and her employer, the associate pastor, made sure she was properly recognized. After a while, he went further, occasionally complimenting her on her appearance and randomly stopping to thank her just for doing her job. Basically, he began giving her the kind of extra attention Ron didn't seem to know she needed.

Over time and without her really knowing how it happened, Nina found she cared more for the pastor's approval than she did for Ron's. She bought clothes that pleased the pastor's taste because she knew he would notice, and she began consulting him before she made decisions. Despite Ron's best efforts, a vacuum remained in Nina's life—a vacuum the abusive pastor used to increase his own status and self-esteem. The marriage began to crumble, and a bewildered Ron worked desperately and futilely to salvage his perfect life.

Now, don't think for a moment that I'm excusing these abusive pastors. I am saying that, by leaving room for the abusive authority to take over, these two husbands failed to protect their families. A true shepherd, though, would have worked to help David and Ron become godly men who could truly lead their households. What happened to their families was evil and sprang the self-promoting wickedness of abusive leadership.

Often leaders like this won't even wait for a "hole" to open up in the families under them. If there is no place for them to work, they'll set out to make one. Remember what we said about how authority abusers need the people under them? Because they need others to help them, they will go to great lengths to keep a family under their influence.

Worst of all is when an authority abuser deliberately sets out to win the heart of a family member. An abusive pastor won the heart of David's wife by fulfilling the spiritual needs

David could not. He won the heart of David's daughter by giving her more of what she wanted (personal freedom) than her father thought wise. In every case, an abuser will seek to one-up the rest of the family in order to win over his target. He might buy his secretary the car her husband couldn't afford, even if her husband just purchased her second-choice car. Or he might give a young man a place on the worship team, even though his parents feel his time should be devoted to education. It takes a strong marriage and a strong family, to stand up under the attack of an abuser determined to drain their life like the juice from a battery.

> What God has joined together, let not man separate.

Making a Hole

If a family is healthy and not open to the abuser's influence, the abuser's first step is often to twist the teaching that a person's first love belongs to God. (See Revelation 2:4.) These teachers almost always brush aside what the Bible says about a man and his wife becoming one flesh.

> *And He answered and said to them, "Have you not read that He who made them at the beginning 'made them male and female,' and said, 'For this reason a man shall leave his father and mother and be joined to his wife, and the two shall become one flesh'? So then, they are no longer two but one flesh. Therefore what God has joined together, let not man separate."* (Matthew 19:4–6)

God used the term *"one flesh"* to describe what happens when two people leave their own agendas and influences to live entirely within the marriage. They need to sacrifice, whenever necessary, their personal objectives in order to minister to each other. Their focus is on the vision God has for them—the vision they should share as if they were the same person.

Jezebel teachers usually argue that this joining is merely physical, though, that a married couple remains two people in spirit; they use the Revelation 2:4 reference to God as our "first love" as support for this belief. I've even heard it taught that, before God presented Eve to Adam, He first "knew" her—both physically and spiritually—Himself! There is no scriptural reason to think God did any such thing. The real reason that the Jezebel spirit wants to separate spouses is because it makes them easier to control. Haven't we all heard the phrase, "Divide and conquer"?

Yet somehow these false teachers make it sound very plausible. "If you really love God more than anything else, you will follow Him no matter what anyone thinks, even your spouse," they say.

What angers me is that this teaching completely ignores God's righteousness! How could a righteous God break His own laws? If He said it is sinful to dissolve a marriage, how could He rightfully break one up? It's no good to say He is God, and "His ways are higher than our ways". The Bible says He is higher than we, that His righteousness is purer than ours; but to say that His righteous plans could be some-thing totally different than ours is ridiculous because His righteousness is the standard we use to determine ours! This one lie opens the door to a giant crypt full of ghastly things.

The first thing this false separation does is to create the possibility that God would call one spouse in one direction and the other spouse in another. (Some churches actually advocate divorce as "God's will" for situations like this.)

Authority Abusers

This lie is almost a guarantee that the authority abuser will be able to hold on to at least part of a family. You see, after having drilled this evil, icy wedge between marriage partners, the abuser doesn't really have to worry if the man of the house becomes suspicious or righteously indignant about the abuser's actions. The husband might even decide to leave the abusive church, but his wife won't go with him. If the abuser has convinced her that God wants her to stay, she will leave her husband and cleave to the ministry—in direct perversion of Jesus' command.

This kind of situation actually helps the authority abuser more than a healthy family does! A man or woman who has abandoned his or her spouse for an abusive ministry will be extra needy and have something to prove. That person will pour herself out, supporting the abusive leader in ways no healthy individual would. Playing the role of an advisor and protector, the abuser gets to soak up all her love and attention at no cost to himself.

> The husband might leave the abusive church, but his wife won't go with him.

Another thing this false separation between husband and wife creates is the possibility that one partner is more "spiritual" than the other. If the abusive leader cannot convince his victim that God is purposely separating her from her husband "for the kingdom's sake," he may begin telling her that her husband is simply walking away from God. Often the abuser will seem very compassionate. He will tell her, "Your husband has such a calling of God on his life, such an anointing! He could be a world-changer, an absolute dynamo for God! I love his spirit...but...if only he didn't have such trouble submitting to authority."

A steady diet of this kind of talk will eventually convince a woman that her husband has a rebellious heart and is wasting his God-given talents. By the time he leaves the abusive ministry, she may be ready to divorce him. Again this plays right into the abuser's hands; for every gifted man he loses, the abuser gains the fanatical devotion of an equally gifted woman (or vice versa).

It doesn't help that most churches today have an activity or two going on every single night of the week. Not that I'm against activities; I think it's good for people to get together during the week and healthy for them to fellowship and minister with each other. The problem is when an abusive authority starts making people feel guilty for missing even one meeting during the week. What happens then is that families begin to disintegrate. Couples don't spend time together because they are organizing and attending their own special programs. Kids and teenagers don't spend time with their parents because they're packed off somewhere with their peer group and a youth pastor. An abusive church completely replaces the family—and we wonder why families break down!

Even worse, abusive ministries replace the family then sequester men off from women, and kids and teens off from their parents. A man doesn't have time to be advised by his wife, and he has no opportunity to teach her what God is teaching him as Paul instructed: *"Husbands, love your wives, even as Christ also loved the church, and gave himself for it; that he might sanctify and cleanse it with the washing of water by the word"* (Ephesians 5:25–26). There is no opportunity for children to learn from adults except the abuser's hand-picked "spiritual leaders." A whole generation can grow up under an authority abuser and never be equipped to know that something is wrong!

Authority Abusers

Stand Up!

In chapter four we examined how the Jezebel spirit loves to override the God-given order of authority. When king Ahab wanted to make inroads on Naboth's family inheritance, Naboth stood as a godly man should and refused to let it happen. But Jezebel was at work in Ahab's life, and she provided the deception and "muscle" to override Naboth's authority. The only way Naboth could have escaped her was to have somehow transported his vineyard out of Israel, away from her influence.

Obviously he couldn't cart a piece of real estate around with him. But the inheritance that God has given you is not in land; as Paul said, *"The kingdom of God is not eating and drinking, but righteousness and peace and joy in the Holy Spirit"* (Romans 14:17). In other words, God's kingdom is not about tangible assets—it's about the hearts and souls of his people. As such, you can protect your inheritance.

Matthew 18:15–17 gives us guidelines about what to do when someone sins against us. If you have recognized your leader's behavior as abusive, you are responsible to confront him and give him the chance to change. Jesus said that, *"If he hears you, you have gained your brother"* (v. 15). But if you follow all of God's instructions for communicating with the abuser and he refuses to change his ways, Jesus said, *"Let him be to you like a heathen and a tax collector"* (v. 17).

In other words, pack up your vineyard and get out of Jezebel's reach! Don't stay where an authority abuser can pick at the walls of your inheritance and hammer at the foundation of your family. Get out from under the abusive ministry and away from the satanic influence. Abuse is never God's will for your family, and He has given the head of every household the authority to prevent it.

Chapter Seven

Domestic Dictatorships

The platoon of Marines was clustered in a small grove of trees. Just across the field lay an enemy stronghold. Nobody knew how many people were inside. They couldn't even be sure they remained unnoticed as they sneaked down the hillside to where they now were.

Stan Jones took a step backward, bumping into Smith who banged the back of Jones' helmet with his fist.

"Watch where you're going, stupid!" Smith yelled.

"Hey, you were in my way!"

"Now look, you two," John raised a hand in warning. "Knock it off. We need to get across that field and into the trees as quietly as we can."

"No, you look," Smith growled. "You're not in charge. Kravitz was, and he's not here now. We rank as high as you, and I say that this looks like a minefield. We need to flank them."

"Kravitz left me in charge, Smith," John spoke icily. "Stand down, or I'll knock you down."

"Try it," Smith challenged.

John did. Smith fell. Smith got back up, and this time John fell. In an instant the entire group of men was a melee of swinging fists and boots. They were so preoccupied with the fight they didn't even notice the shadowy figures surrounding them until machine-gun fire cut them all down.

Seems ridiculous, doesn't it? No one would be foolish enough to indulge in a petty power struggle that close to a deadly enemy, would they? Sadly, I see this kind of foolishness almost every day in marriages. *"Marriage is honorable among all,"* according to Hebrews 13:4. Where is the honor, though, when so many marriages are ending in divorce? Although the two are supposed to become one, they often remain separate entities, fighting for the throne of power through manipulation and control; this is a sad abuse of the quest for authority. Husbands seek to control wives, wives seek to manipulate husbands, while the enemy seeks to destroy them both. Often couples are so preoccupied with their own struggles they don't even realize the fallen world is trying to tear them apart.

Many marriages that God created to annihilate the enemy have found themselves at the brunt of enemy fire, possessing the weapons to defeat that enemy but lacking the readiness to draw those weapons in defense. The battle becomes most tragic when one half of the couple begins abusing his or her God-given authority over the other or over the entire family.

In our book, *Crazy House Sane House*, my wife discusses many of the challenges we experienced early in our marriage. We married as soon as she graduated from high school and found out the hard way that there's more to marriage than simply , "I do." I grew up with an abusive and dogmatic father; it wasn't until after my wife and I got married, though, that these tendencies began awakening in me, and I began acting out my father's abusive habits with my wife as target. Screaming or simply not speaking to each other at all constituted our communication while I sought to control my wife with my dominant personality. I refused to respond when she tried communicating her concerns, and eventually she began to shut down as well. Though we lived in the same house, we became two separate entities. Even the children began looking at me as "the strange man in mommy's house."

> In the same house, we became two separate entities.

Using the "silent treatment" instead of simply telling your partner your needs is a dangerous game to play. Although most only resort to the silent treatment when all else fails and communication has produced no results, it's still a product of deceit that only worsens the problem and complicates the situation.

Early in my marriage whenever my wife did not like the way things were going, I would just shut down. My attitude was, "I'm the man of the house, and that settles it!" This dominating way of handling our problems left no room for communication, only control. Because my wife had no way to process her feelings and no outlet for expression, she began releasing her emotions through yelling. With a smug look, I'd simply look at her and ask, "What are you yelling about?" making her feel guilty for refusing to see things my way. We were definitely in a war—with each other. The outcome of such shutting down is not resolution, but bitterness; many women today are bitter because certain men, who accept only a one-sided view of every situation and refuse to communicate, have treated them so negligently.

As I began relinquishing my "throne" of control, we were met by one more challenge. Because I had traveled a lot and was often away from home, my wife and children had formed their own bond and special way of doing things. Consequently, I was often like a guest or stranger in my home. Whenever I went to the refrigerator, for instance, my children would run to my wife and say, "Mama, *he's* in the refrigerator," as if I were a guest and not the father of the home. My wife would have to explain that it was okay for Daddy to get into the refrigerator. Once I began spending more time at home, they relaxed, welcomed my presence, and we enjoyed spending time with each other.

Because my wife had created her own environment to deal with my absence and with the emotions she'd started to suppress, it was difficult at first for her to relinquish her control in our relationship. Her thoughts were, "If I let go, he's going to win, and I want God to punish Him for what He's done to me." She explains, though, that as I became more active in the home and relinquished my "control," after we began working together as a team, releasing her control became an honor, not a task. Because we both wanted our marriage badly enough, we each stepped aside and allowed the other to contribute to the marriage instead of focusing on who was going to "win" the next battle.

So many homes are in trouble today because one wants to lead and the other refuses to follow bad leadership. Marriage, though, is not a compound for ungodly control and manipulation; it is a refuge for support and encouragement. Though marriage will—and should—experience its challenges, it is a place of unification where both parties are committed to securing the fulfillment and growth of each other's future, enjoying the fruits of two who have become one along the way.

"Thank God I'm Not a Woman"

Sadly, the church has done more to demean women than any other institution in history. Back in the 1300s, Geoffrey Chaucer wrote what became the oldest surviving fiction ever written in the English language. In one of his stories, a woman from the city of Bath complains at great length about the typical religious attitude toward women. It seems that in her day religious leaders wrote whole books trying to convince people that women could not be trusted and should be kept under tight rein by their husbands. She complains that her husband wouldn't even buy her nice clothing because he thought it would encourage her sinful imagination!

This suspicious, dominant male behavior is a far cry from the way Jesus Himself treated women while He was on earth. The Hebrew society at that time was so man-centered that, at every synagogue service, the Hebrew men prayed, "Blessed art thou, O Lord, who hast not made me a woman." Yet when a woman who had been a prostitute anointed Jesus with oil and washed his feet with tears of repentance, He defended her actions, telling critics,

> *Assuredly, I say to you, wherever this gospel is preached in the whole world, what this woman has done will also be told as a memorial to her.* (Matthew 26:13)

In another instance, a woman with an unstoppable hemorrhage broke several Old Testament laws while searching for her healing. She sneaked through a crowd of people and actually touched Jesus, even though she was ceremonially unclean and should have been stoned for her audacity. Because of her faith, though, she was healed immediately. Jesus—who was rushing to heal the daughter of an important man—stopped everything to make the woman "'fess up" in front of the whole crowd. He didn't do this to punish her, though; when she identified herself, Jesus said tenderly, *"Daughter, be of good cheer; your faith has made you well. Go in peace"* (Luke 8:48).

I'm hardly the first person to point this out, but this bears repeating, too: when Jesus rose from the dead, before He returned to the Father, He didn't immediately show himself to any of "the boys," not even John the beloved! Instead He appeared to a young lady whose love for Him kept her at His tomb after the disciples had given up and gone home.

> *But Mary stood outside by the tomb weeping, and as she wept she stooped down and looked into the tomb. And she saw two angels in white sitting, one at the head and the other at the feet, where the body of Jesus had lain....Now...she turned around and saw Jesus standing there, and did not know that it was Jesus. Jesus said to her, "Woman, why*

are you weeping? Whom are you seeking?" She, supposing Him to be the gardener, said to Him, "Sir, if You have carried Him away, tell me where You have laid Him, and I will take Him away." Jesus said to her, "Mary!" She turned and said to Him, "Rabboni!" (which is to say, Teacher). Jesus said to her, "Do not cling to Me, for I have not yet ascended to My Father; but go to My brethren and say to them, 'I am ascending to My Father and your Father, and to My God and your God.'" (John 20:11–17)

It's clear Jesus respected and honored women. During His day, one of the most popular Bible scholars taught that a man could divorce his wife if she upset him for any reason—including burning his dinner! Jesus disagreed:

The Pharisees also came to Him, testing Him, and saying to Him, "Is it lawful for a man to divorce his wife for just any reason?" And He answered and said to them, "Have you not read that He who made them at the beginning 'made them male and female,' **Jesus treated women with an unusual level of respect.** *and said, 'For this reason a man shall leave his father and mother and be joined to his wife, and the two shall become one flesh'? So then, they are no longer two but one flesh. Therefore what God has joined together, let not man separate." They said to Him, "Why then did Moses command to give a certificate of divorce, and to put her away?" He said to them, "Moses, because of the hardness of your hearts, permitted you to divorce your wives, but from the beginning it was not so. And I say to you, whoever divorces his wife, except for sexual immorality, and marries another, commits adultery."* (Matthew 19:3–9)

An open-minded reading of the four Gospels will clearly show Jesus treated women with a level of respect

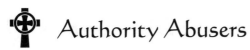

and gentleness unusual for the time. Why then, have his followers been so infamous for their poor treatment of women?

The Jezebel spirit takes every chance to promote itself, especially when someone else will end up in a more easily controlled position. But this poor treatment of women has a lot to do with a misunderstanding, too, I think. For a lot of people, "Submit to authority" means the exact same thing as, "Be a doormat."

Family Authority

Wives, submit to your own husbands, as to the Lord. For the husband is head of the wife, as also Christ is head of the church; and He is the Savior of the body. Therefore, just as the church is subject to Christ, so let the wives be to their own husbands in everything. (Ephesians 5:22–24)

Let's go back to the purpose of godly authority: **to nurture and cultivate whatever is placed under it.** This definition doesn't allow for a wife to be a doormat while her husband is a set of heavy boots. Look at the rest of the apostle Paul's instructions:

Husbands, love your wives, just as Christ also loved the church and gave Himself for her, that He might sanctify and cleanse her with the washing of water by the word, that He might present her to Himself a glorious church, not having spot or wrinkle or any such thing, but that she should be holy and without blemish. (vv. 25–27)

Husbands are to love their wives just as Christ loved the church. And how did Christ love the church? He gave Himself for her. Well that's simple enough. Even a dominating husband would die for his wife if he had to.

But wait—is that what "giving your life" always means? Is that how you gave your life to Christ? Of course not. You're still breathing, sitting there, reading this book. You're very much alive; but your life isn't your own, is it? If you sincerely committed yourself to Christ, you gave Him permission to inconvenience you. You promised to give your life to Him, moment by moment. You see, Paul wasn't talking about a husband giving his life for his wife in some heroic, snap-decision moment; he said God demands the much harder sacrifice, day-by-day, moment-by-moment sacrificial love:

> *Love is patient, love is kind. It does not envy, it does not boast, it is not proud. It is not rude, it is not self-seeking, it is not easily angered, it keeps no record of wrongs.*
> (1 Corinthians 13:4–6, NIV)

And Paul wasn't finished! He wrote,

> *So husbands ought to love their own wives as their own bodies; he who loves his wife loves himself. For no one ever hated his own flesh, but nourishes and cherishes it, just as the Lord does the church.* (Ephesians 5:28–29)

And here we are, back at the Garden of Eden where Adam was given authority so that he would cultivate everything under his care. This is how a healthy marriage is to be.

I told the following story in *Crazy House, Sane House*, to illustrate how much fun it can be to bless your wife's development:

"Some time ago I asked my wife, 'What do you want to do with your life?' I encouraged her to set goals and to pursue them. She has many gifts, and it is up to me to encourage her to develop them. A few weeks later, she came to me and said, 'I want to go back to school.' I was pleased with her decision. Now my wife has an accounting business in which she handles millions of dollars, manages properties, makes sure the bills are paid on time, does payroll, pays insurance, and all kinds of things. It is not enough for me just to acknowledge Jeannie; I must invest in her life. I feel free to invest in her because I feel secure in my own position before God. I have reaped the benefits of my investment countless times."

I have found that the more I encourage Jeannie to grow and the more I build her confidence in the gifts God has given her, the stronger our marriage gets. And as she becomes a more capable person, I become a more capable minister! Her growth really is my growth because we are dedicated to the same vision. Back when I was "king of my household," I was stressed-out and always on the run. It was too much for one person to handle! From where we are now it is easy to see how badly I was crippling myself by starving Jeannie of the opportunities and encouragement she needed. No man who wants to keep his wife "in her place" has any idea how much joy and strength he could find by letting her stretch her wings!

> *Joy and strength come from letting her stretch her wings.*

"[Love] *always protects, always trusts, always hopes, always perseveres*" (1 Corinthians 13:7, NIV).

Enter the Dictator

We've already talked about how subtle authority abuse can be in the context of the church. Let me emphasize: The abuse of authority can be more deceitful and more difficult to spot in marriage than anywhere else. This is mostly because marriage is a such an intense relationship; there is just that much more opportunity for a man's sinful nature to make a mess of things.

Most people think an abusive husband is an alcoholic or a drug addict; some are. When they envision abusive husbands, they think of raised voices and the sound of breaking glass filtering through thin walls late at night. Trust me; that does happen far too often. Such abuse is blatant abuse, and anyone who can think clearly about the situation knows the woman should get out of the relationship. There are many forms of marital abuse, though, that don't look nearly as ugly as physical abuse— yet do just as much damage to a woman's spirit.

When a man deprives his wife of fellowship, approval, and physical affection in order to starve her into submission, he disobeys his mandate to love and cultivate her. I call this *the abuse of neglect*, and such behavior is a rebellion against the very reasons God gave the man authority over his wife.

I have described some of the effects my own icy stranglehold had on Jeannie, and I can assure you the damage to her heart was much worse than it looks on paper. I feel my past behavior gives me the right to be forceful on this subject since I speak passionately from a humble heart that's learned its lesson the hard way. My wife has forgiven me, and, thanks to God's incredible grace, there is no lasting scar on her heart or our relationship. The fact remains, though, that for a time I abused the authority I had over her—I was an abusive husband, although I doubt anyone around us would have guessed it.

Many Christian men—abusive and otherwise—like to quote 1 Corinthians 7:3-5 to their wives. Here Paul was talking about marriage and the responsibilities each partner has to the other:

> *The husband should fulfill his marital duty to his wife, and likewise the wife to her husband. The wife's body does not belong to her alone but also to her husband. In the same way, the husband's body does not belong to him alone but also to his wife. Do no deprive each other except by mutual consent and for a time, so that you may devote yourselves to prayer.* (NIV)

As I'm sure you can imagine, many husbands have used this passage while trying to wring more sexual intimacy out of their wives. I could say a lot about the proper usage of this passage, but right now I just want to reverse the usual spin people take on it.

Now, you can pick up any book, newspaper, or magazine article about marital sex and find that all the experts, Christian and non-Christian alike, agree on one thing: Enjoyment of sexual intimacy is almost completely physical for men and nearly all emotional for women. There is nothing wrong with either side—this is how God designed things, and it works beautifully in a healthy marriage. Let me phrase things a different way, though: for most women, the best part of sex happens before they ever reach the bed. The loving look in her husband's eye, the intimate conversations, and the act of sharing a life together are necessary ingredients for making a wife feel sexually fulfilled.

For women, the best part of sex happens before they reach the bed.

So I ask you, who's defrauding whom of their *"marital duty"* when a husband uses the abuse of neglect to get his way? It's not the wife shortchanging the husband, in such cases, but the husband shortchanging the wife.

There are other, more aggressive forms of abuse than the abuse of neglect. Because the controlling aspects of the Jezebel spirit always operate out of the same self-serving motivation, these forms of abuse look a lot like what we've discussed in previous chapters. Does your husband insist your entire relationship with God be filtered through him? Are you afraid to make mistakes in front of him for fear you will be made fun of? Do you have to be extra careful to keep things "just so," so he won't get crabby? When you talk to him about his faults, does he get angry?

Many husbands don't know they are abusing their authority. Selfishness doesn't look nearly so evil when it happens in the family den as it does when it crosses a pastor's desk. Manipulation might not seem very ugly when it buys a husband a little extra time to work on his golf game, even though such manipulation in a church setting might be easier to identify as abuse. As I've told you, it took both the Holy Spirit's work and my wife's steadfast determination to get through to me, to help me see where I was abusing authority in my home. Had my heart been much harder, I don't know if I could have seen how wrong I was. It was a hard lesson to accept, and changing my behavior was at first a bitter pill to swallow.

I don't want to overlook the horrible evil of physical and verbal abuse in marriage. The truth is, though, these are only a continuation of the traits we have discussed here. The spiritual influence and mental stance behind aggressive abuse starts with an often nonviolent struggle for control, and I don't want that fact to get lost in the graphic retelling of domestic horror stories.

Authority Abusers

Remember, Jesus never looked at the surface of things; He dug deeper to the root of the problem, plunged further until He reached the heart of the matter. When a young man asked Jesus how to get into the kingdom of heaven, for instance, Jesus didn't bring up any of the fellow's obvious shortcomings. The young man told Jesus he had always kept the Law of Moses, ever since he was a child. If I had been Jesus, I think I would have had something to say to this guy about lying! But Jesus zeroed in on the young man's biggest problem, on the one thing he loved more than God—his money.

We see Jesus going beneath the surface of things, too, whenever He taught we should be most concerned about sin's source: "if a man looks at a woman lustfully, he has committed adultery with her"—and should deal ruthlessly with that source—"if your hand leads you to sin, cut it off." (See Matthew 5:28–30.)

The absolute light of God's truth will illuminate the darkest closet as well as the corner behind the couch. But it's behind the couch that we often neglect, so that corner stays dirtier than many closets. As Jesus looked beneath surfaces, so too must we delve deep into the underlying causes of abuse.

Chapter Eight

Rebels and Rabble-Rousers

Therefore I exhort first of all that supplications, prayers, intercessions, and giving of thanks be made for all men, for kings and all who are in authority, that we may lead a quiet and peaceable life in all godliness and reverence.
—1 Timothy 2:1–2

I t wouldn't be fair to talk about leaders who abuse their authority over others without addressing followers who abuse the leaders in authority over them. I don't intend to spend much time on the topic, though, because I don't think it's necessary. Over the years, leaders of all kinds have made strong cases for why they should have the respect and submission of the people under their authority. But in order to promote a balanced view of authority, let's chat about rebels for a moment.

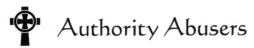 Authority Abusers

Remember our discussion of Lucifer's rebellion against God? The prophet Isaiah, under influence of the Holy Spirit, mourned his fall hundreds of years later.

> *How you are fallen from heaven, O Lucifer, son of the morning! How you are cut down to the ground, You who weakened the nations! For you have said in your heart: "I will ascend into heaven, I will exalt my throne above the stars of God; I will also sit on the mount of the congregation on the farthest sides of the north; I will ascend above the heights of the clouds, I will be like the Most High."*
> (Isaiah 14:12–14)

Notice the five claims this prideful archangel made; I call them the five "I wills"—I will ascend into heaven, I will exalt my throne, I will sit on the mount, I will ascend above the clouds, I will be like the Most High. When you boil these down you find that Lucifer simply couldn't stand that God was greater than him. Perhaps we shouldn't be blamed for feeling the same way sometimes, right? After all, it's really a very democratic idea. No one should be better than anyone else. No one should tell anyone else what to do. People should talk about thing and compromise, right?

Well, that makes for pretty good civil government. But that's not how God set His kingdom to work, and that's not how the world in general operates. Authority is not solely derived from how talented an individual is, how qualified a person looks, or how available someone is to do a job no one else can do. Authority comes with position. As Paul said, *"Let every soul be subject to the governing authorities. For there is no authority except from God, and the authorities that exist are appointed by God"* (Romans 13:1).

Aaron and Miriam, Moses' brother and sister, once got confused about this very point. *"So they said, 'Has the*

Lord *indeed spoken only through Moses? Has He not spoken through us also?'"* (Numbers 12:2) They were upset that Moses—whom they knew was imperfect—got so much authority over things when he wasn't the only person who had heard from God. They thought his authority came from his ability, and they knew they were nearly as gifted as he was. As God made very clear to them, though, Moses' authority was simply a gift of grace: *"I speak with him face to face, even plainly, and not in dark sayings; and he sees the form of the Lord"* (v. 8). God took Aaron and Miriam's rebellion so seriously that the cloud of His presence left the tabernacle, and he struck Miriam with leprosy until they repented.

I think it is important to notice *when* God dealt with Miriam's and Aaron's attitudes. He didn't wait until they had decided to ask for Moses' resignation; He called them on the carpet as soon as they began criticizing their leader. I've told you that I go out of my way to be accessible to my people. Part of the reason for this is that I don't want them talking behind my back—for their sakes! As the situation with Aaron and Miriam shows, God clearly doesn't take kindly to that kind of behavior. (Now it's important to notice here that Moses didn't take matters into his own hands but let God take care of it. The account says, *"The man Moses was very humble, more than all men who were on the face of the earth"* (v. 3). Moses let God handle authority issues of this sort.)

> God called them on the carpet as soon as they criticized their leader.

Sadly, criticizing leadership has become so commonplace that people joke about having "roast preacher" for Sunday dinner. And some wives gossip so badly about their husbands that to figure out what kind of men they really

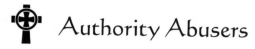

are, you could balance how much their best friends like them against how awful their wives' friends think they are. There are many reasons for such disrespectful treatment of authority, but they usually boil down to two motivations.

1. Get Mad at God, Stone the Preacher.

When the children of Israel left slavery in Egypt, the Lord led them toward the Red Sea. Pharaoh, who was either an unusually resilient or amazingly stupid individual, rethought the decision he had made to let the Hebrews go. He had made his decision under the most extreme kinds of duress imaginable and now concluded he had done the wrong thing in releasing the Hebrews from slavery. So he gathered his best armored division (that's what chariots were in those days) and set out to recapture the Israelites. When he found them, they were camped facing the Red Sea. On either side of them were steep rock cliffs.

Now every Israelite saw the exact same thing Pharaoh did—and for them it was terrifying. It was like the end of an old Western: on one side, a powerful attacking force; and on the other, our heroes trapped in the end of a box canyon. They had trusted God with everything they had, and now it looked like He was going to feed them to the Egyptians for an early-morning snack. Understandably, they were quite upset!

Here is where they went wrong: instead of crying out to God, asking Him for an explanation and some help (as Moses had done a few hours later), they turned against their earthly leader. They accused Moses of deceiving them or, at the very least, of being a grossly incompetent leader whom they should never have trusted. They decided that, since they were all going to die or be enslaved, Moses should be executed while they still had the chance. They would have stoned Moses if God had not intervened.

I think a lot of Christians live in those moments before the parting of the Red Sea. So often when they become disappointed with God, they blame their hurt feelings on the pastor. If God does not heal them when they expect Him to, they accuse the pastor of preaching a lie. If they tithe faithfully without getting the riches they expected in return, they demand that the pastor explain why God isn't blessing them. And if they don't feel God's anointing in services like they think they should, they begin murmuring that the pastor must be an "old wineskin" who is quenching the Spirit.

2. I Could Do Better.

A real favorite of the Jezebel spirit is the idea that "I could do (*fill in the blank*) better than the person in authority is doing it." Remember how Jezebel got the vineyard of Naboth for her husband? She usurped the king's authority by sending orders in Ahab's name, ordering that Naboth be executed on false charges. Her reasoning was that if Ahab couldn't get the job done, she'd do it for him.

This motivation is often at work in marriages and families as well as churches. Almost everyone knows a man who is "whipped"—that is, completely submissive to his wife. She gets her way in almost everything and makes all the decisions. Do you think she would admit that is controlling—or worse, acting in the Jezebel spirit? Of course not! I expect you could ask one hundred of these rebellious wives why they run their households, and every one would answer that it's because their husbands do a terrible job of things if given the chance.

Authority Abusers

Now it is true that abuse fosters abuse. When a woman has been hurt by a man, she will often vow never to let it happen again. For most wounded women this means controlling every part of their own lives, including their husbands. Although this variation seems much more understandable, it still means the woman cannot or will not trust the authority God has put over her.

Once this idea gets planted in a person's head, it can be almost impossible to get rid of. I have seen an entire church staff at war with the pastor and each other, all because a few people wanted the power to "do things right." Jesus once told a story in which an estate manager refused to do anything with the money in his care because he believed his boss was cold-hearted and didn't handle profits correctly. His three coworkers did their best to manage their responsibilities, and, at the business meeting, they were each awarded with a higher position in the company. But the man who "knew better" than his boss was fired on the spot and fined for damages! Jesus was saying—among other things—that no one who refuses to submit to his or her authority will be trusted with responsibilities in the kingdom of heaven.

> The man who "knew better" than his boss was fired on the spot.

I have heard stories that would curl your hair—or straighten it out stiff if it's naturally curly. I was once told how the head intercessor of a neighboring church became convinced her pastor was not following God's plan for that church. She began to pray that God would set him straight, but that is not all she did. This woman, in her efforts to do better than the leadership was doing, began whispering in the ears of people on the worship team and of the associate ministers. She was well-respected and had a sincere love for the Lord, so people listened to her. It was only a matter of months before it became obvious the pastor was moving in one direction while most of the congregation and people in leadership were moving in another. Before much time had passed, the board asked the senior pastor to resign and voted the associate pastor into his place. The head intercessor had complete control over this man and thus was able to run the church. The former pastor left heartbroken, victim of the sting of Jezebel.

The most frightening thing about stories like these is that they end with authority being passed on to someone who does not understand it at all. When Jezebel installed Baal worship in Israel, she won indisputable victory by murdering every prophet of the Lord she could find. I'm sure that, in her mind, the ends justified the means. But as the murder of Naboth shows, she did not change once she had the power she wanted! The same holds true for every abusive person who usurps authority. If a person uses manipulation and deceit to earn a place of influence, you can be sure that person will use manipulation and deceit to control the people under him or her.

In short, people who abuse the authority they are *under* will abuse the people they have authority *over.* The cycle of authority abuse will continue; and as we saw in the story of the Red Sea, only God has the power to break it.

Chapter Nine

Restoration of Proper Authority

So I will restore to you the years that the swarming locust has
eaten, the crawling locust, the consuming locust, and the chewing
locust...You shall eat in plenty and be satisfied, and praise the
name of the LORD your God, who has dealt wondrously with you;
and My people shall never be put to shame.
—Joel 2:25–26

Going down to a Samaritan city, Philip proclaimed the Message of the Messiah. When the people heard what he had to say and saw the miracles, the clear signs of God's action, they hung on his every word, Many who could neither stand nor walk were healed that day. The evil spirits protested loudly as they were sent on their way. And what joy in the city!

Authority Abusers

Previous to Philip's arrival, a certain Simon had practiced magic in the city, posing as a famous man and dazzling all the Samaritans with his wizardry He had them all, from little children to old men, eating out of his hand. They all thought he had supernatural powers, and called him "the Great Wizard." He had been around a long time, and everyone was more or less in awe of him.

But when Philip came to town announcing the news of God's kingdom and proclaiming the name of Jesus Christ, they forgot Simon and were baptized, becoming believers right and left. Even Simon himself believed and was baptized. From that moment he was like Philip's shadow, so fascinated with all the God-signs and miracles that he wouldn't leave Philip's side.

When the apostles in Jerusalem received the report that Samaria had accepted God's Message, they sent Peter and John down to pray for them to receive the Holy Spirit. Up to this point they had only been baptized in the name of the Master Jesus; the Holy Spirit hadn't yet fallen on them. Then the apostles laid their hands on them and they did receive the Holy Spirit.

When Simon saw that the apostles by merely laying on hands, conferred the Spirit, he pulled out his money, excited, and said, "Sell me your secret! Show me how you did that! How much you want? Name your price!"

Peter said, "To hell with your money! And you along with it! Why, that's unthinkable—trying to buy God's gift! You'll never be part of what God is doing by striking bargains and offering bribes. Change your ways—and now! Ask the Master to forgive you for trying to use God to make money. I can see this is an old habit with you; you reek with money-lust."

Restoration of Proper Authority

"Oh!" said Simon, "pray for me! Pray to the Master that nothing like that will ever happen to me!"
(Acts 8:5–24, MESSAGE)

Most often this text is used as a lesson against greed or to teach the importance of pure motives. And no wonder! Simon was one of the "best" authority abusers you've ever heard of. For years he held an entire town under his thumb. He had them all convinced he was the servant of some god, maybe even a god himself. Even once he was converted and the abused townspeople were freed from his influence, he couldn't help seeing the Holy Spirit's power as a way to become influential. What I love most about this story, though, is that Simon changed. Not only does the account tell us that people can be freed from abuse by accepting Jesus; seemingly incorrigible authority abusers can change, too.

At least, that's how I read it. By the end of the story, Simon seems genuinely repentant, and I can't find anywhere in the Bible where God rejected true repentance. Since the Bible doesn't say otherwise, I have to assume that, following his strong lesson in humility, Simon learned to truly love the people around him. And since, as Romans 13:10 says, *"Love does no wrong to a neighbor; therefore love is the fulfilling of the law,"* I believe Simon was freed from being an authority abuser.

The weight of Scripture teaches that the Spirit of God can free anyone—abused or abuser—and restore that person to a life of wholeness and blessing. God is the only one who can do this. He is the only One capable of not just restoring what the devil has killed or destroyed, but of also returning it with more abundance than we can even imagine. Die; then God will come. Die to worry, doubt, and carnality— watch God come and restore life more abundantly.

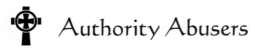

Nevertheless death reigned from Adam to Moses, even over them that had not sinned after the similitude of Adam's transgression, who is the figure of him that was to come. But not as the offence, so also is the free gift. For if through the offence of one many be dead, much more the grace of God, and the gift by grace, which is by one man, Jesus Christ, hath abounded unto many. And not as it was by one that sinned, so is the gift: for the judgment was by one to condemnation, but the free gift is of many offences unto justification. For if by one man's offence death reigned by one; much more they which receive abundance of grace and of the gift of righteousness shall reign in life by one, Jesus Christ.) (Romans 5:12–17)

In the womb you were shaped in sin, conceived in iniquity—and came out a sinner. It's not a person's will to be that way; they were just "made" that way. *"For if through the offence of one many be dead, much more the grace of God, and the gift by grace, which is by one man, Jesus Christ, hath abounded unto many"* (verse 15). Though worded differently, this verse is a repeat of John 10:10. God says, "Okay, you sinned, and the penalty is death. The thief came to you; he stole from you and robbed you, but I'm going to give you a free gift, and the free gift is life." God says, "I'm going to resurrect you out of a mind-set that has kept you bound. I'm going to set you free—not in your own righteousness, but in the righteousness of God. *"And not as it was by one that sinned, so is the gift: for the judgment was by one to condemnation, gift is of many offences unto justification"* (Romans 5:16). One person sinned, and sin fell upon all, but the God of "much more" consoles and restores us by promising, "I'll not only forgive you for the sins you committed just by being born; but also any sins you commit after being born, My grace is powerful enough to combat those as well."

Restoration of Proper Authority

Grace is God's commitment to bombard the nation of the flesh and execute His rescue mission to free you from the enemy's elaborate snares. He alone, then, justifies you by faith—forgives you, cleans you up, and shreds the evidence of your past transgressions. That is why Romans 8:1 declares, *"There is therefore now no condemnation to them which are in Christ Jesus."* This verse did not say *conviction,* but rather *condemnation,* which is what others think about you. If you continue going through life worrying about what others think about you, you will continue to miss God. *"For if by one man's offence death reigned by one; much more they which receive abundance of grace and of the gift of righteousness shall reign in life by one, Jesus Christ"* (verse 17). The Bible actually says that the point of receiving the gift of righteousness is where ones release in life is found. The vision for your life will never fully come to fruition as long as you subscribe to guilt and condemnation.

It is the cleansing power of Jesus Christ that makes you feel worthy enough to be blessed. Often we continue to tell people that they're not worthy enough to be blessed, fueling the rejection that might already being lying inside their emotional closet. Instead we sometimes need to tell individuals they're doing a good job so their confidence level can be built to a standard of assurance of themselves in God. I speak from experience; because I suffered rejection as a child, I had to go through a period of growth before I learned how to encourage myself, walk in the Spirit of God, and develop a true relationship with Him for myself. Other Christians play an important part in this growth process.

> *This I say then, Walk in the Spirit, and you shall not fulfil the lust of the flesh.* (Galatians 5:16)

Authority Abusers

Everything that the devil has twisted and taken in your life, you have the power and authority to demand he put back. Every lamp he's overturned in your tidy room of righteousness and peace, he has to set right-side-up again. Although you've made some mistakes in your life, if you continue to seek God and praise Him, He will restore the devastation that canker worms have inflicted on your mind and in your life.

> *The threshing floors shall be full of wheat, and the vats shall overflow with new wine and oil. So I will restore to you the years that the swarming locust has eaten, the crawling locust, the consuming locust, and the chewing locust, My great army which I sent among you. You shall eat in plenty and be satisfied, and praise the name of the LORD your God, who has dealt wondrously with you; and My people shall never be put to shame.* (Joel 2:24–26)

The Lord declares that you are the righteousness of God, bought with a price. Though you're warring with two nations, who you really are will eventually come forth and you'll find that person to be nothing like what the devil tried to convince you was inside. Too many times we believe the voice of Lucifer over the divine destiny God has spoken and ordained for our lives.

> *God is not a man, that He should lie, Nor a son of man, that He should repent. Has He said, and will He not do? Or has He spoken, and will He not make it good?* (Numbers 23:19)

God has already told the principalities that you are anointed; He is not intimidated by what intimidates many others, like your past or your present situation. He knew your ending before your beginning and is not swayed when it appears to others that you're not going to make it.

Some of us are still living off prayers our mothers or grandmothers prayed over us when we were children. God has forgiven us all of some great trespasses and has restored what the enemy said was destroyed forever. If God can forgive us of the offensive acts we've committed, then we in turn should learn to forgive others of their trespasses against us. How can we say we love God and not exercise His gift of forgiveness? You, who were dead in trespasses and sin, the thief came and destroyed; but God came and brought you back to life. God is using your testimony to show the world His grace, His goodness, and His power.

You're not going to enjoy the benefits of a solid relationship with God by continuing to worry about yesterday's experiences by being too afraid to face tomorrow; so thank God for today. He did not begin loving you when you turned from sin and began seeking Him; rather He loved you while you were yet in your sinful "yesterday." He loved you in spite of you. The love of God is not something we deserve. It is a gift, and even when you've blown it, He still loves you and shows up where you are to pull you out of the quagmire of confusion and place your feet upon a solid foundation of stability.

God loved you in spite of you.

Jesus said, *"If you abide in My word, you are My disciples indeed. And you shall know the truth, and the truth shall make you free"* (John 8:31–32). With this book, I am doing my best to help you see the truth about authority abuse. The spirit of Jezebel has been at work in the world for so long that hardly anyone has lived without being brushed by it. Fathers, mothers, pastors, teachers, youth leaders, husbands, wives—people all around us are clawing desperately for control and depending on the manipulation of people instead of on Christ for their security.

I hope that, by the grace of God, this book has enabled you to see any abuse that might be lurking in your life. Simply recognizing that it is there and that it is a perversion of God's plan is a huge step. As we've discussed, abusive leaders usually try to make their victims feel as if the abuse is their fault instead of admitting that it is sin gone haywire. If you can see abuse for what it is, you have taken a major step toward freedom—even if you are the abuser.

Let me strongly urge you: if you have the slightest feeling that you may be trapped in abusive behavior patterns—seek God! Ask Him to show you the true state of your heart. Remember, He takes this with deadly seriousness, but He will never reject a repentant heart. The apostle Paul was a murderer, someone who hated God and fought openly against His people. Yet when he acknowledged he was wrong and surrendered to God, Paul was restored. Not only that, but God also used Paul as one of the most effective servants the kingdom has ever known.

If you have been an abuser:

If you've been an abuser, the very first thing you have to do is accept responsibility. I know many abusers are trying to salvage their lives from the abuse someone has inflicted on them, but that doesn't excuse you. If you want to find the wholeness God has for you, you must face your sin without trying to make it seem any less than it really is; then you need to take it to God. When you ask His forgiveness, you will have to repent. That's an old-school word for "change your mind," or "turn around and go the other way." It is a lot like breaking an addiction to drugs.

I know, because the Lord delivered me from a cocaine habit that, at its worst, cost me about $500 a day. When I first quit, I went cold turkey. This didn't last, because all I had done was dredge up all my willpower to suppress my ever present need for the next fix. I had to quit a second time, this time through a careful detoxification program. Through it, I adopted a life of discipline; I stopped spending time in places where I could buy cocaine if I wanted it, worked on developing good habits to fill the time I used to spend stoned, and began "medicating" myself daily with the Word of God and prayer.

> Medicate yourself every day with prayer and Bible study.

Obviously a daily dose of time with God brought the most powerful change in my life. *"The LORD...inclined to me, and heard my cry. He also brought me up out of a horrible pit, out of the miry clay, And set my feet upon a rock, and established my steps"* (Psalm 40:1–2). But I had to honor the work He was doing by disciplining myself away from old habits.

You must apply the same principles to the "addiction" of authority abuse. Medicate yourself every day with time in prayer and Bible study. Get God's truth into your bloodstream; it will change you. And develop a practice of using less authority than you actually have. Yes, that's what I said—voluntarily cut back on your own authority. The extra humility and discipline will make room for God to work in your heart.

You see, I know that having authority can be kind of fun. If I'm in my office and feeling pretty good about myself, I could tell you, "Hey, watch this." Then I'd bark at one of my assistants, "Kenneth!" (Not his real name, of course.) "Grab me that paper off the table!"

You know what? He'd do it with a smile because that's the kind of authority I have in my office. I don't have to get up for anything I don't want to, but I make a habit of doing my own fetching and carrying whenever I can. You'll never lose by doing a little work instead of flexing your authority.

Finally, as you engage in this life of discipline, get yourself under someone else's authority. Remember what the centurion said to Jesus? That authority must be delegated from above? If you don't have someone over you to whom you can be accountable, you're not a safe person to have in leadership. You simply can't ask people to do what you are unwilling to do. Before Jesus asked us to give Him our lives, He sacrificed His for us. Before you can ask anyone to submit to you, your own will must be submitted to a God-ordained authority.

I know this all sounds pretty simple. I can almost hear someone asking, "So that's all he has to do? An abusive leader can just repent, submit himself, and then discipline his life? That's it?" My answer is, "Yes."

Natural consequences aside (if he broke the law, then that will have to be dealt with), that's all. That's all Jesus ever asks from us. All He wants is all of us. When we reject our sin, come to Him, and truly make Him master of who we are, there is nothing left to give. That's when grace begins to work. I pray that no one who reads this book will put it down without asking God, "What about me? What kind of steward have I been with the authority You've given me?"

And whatever the answer, I pray it will drive you to lean on Him more than ever before.

Restoration of Proper Authority

If you have been a victim:

If you have been a victim, God wants to restore proper authority in your life. I understand that if you are just recognizing how abusive an authority over you has been, restoring authority might not sound like good news. Let me explain how you can start down the path to restoration, though. If you'll come along, I believe that your heart will be healed and ready for whatever God wants to do in your life by the time you reach the end.

Step One: Forgiveness

The first thing you have to do is find the high ground of forgiveness. Climb up out of the muddy, malaria-infested swamp of grudge-holding and rest on the higher plain of forgiveness where the wind of the Holy Spirit can waft away the stench trying to cling to you.

As I've mentioned before, I grew up with an overbearing father who was abusive whenever he wasn't absent. He didn't provide for our family, and he blamed us for most of his problems. My pastor was much like my father. When I was twelve, I met another form of abuse; a thirty-year old woman, one of my mother's friends, sexually molested me while I was at her house. The aggression against me left such a painful scar on my heart that, for years, I only had to close my eyes to be able to see every detail of the room we were in. I remember the music that was playing, and hearing that song can still twist my stomach into knots. I can give you the exact street, house, and apartment number where she lived.

But I don't have to relive the pain from those situations anymore. It did not make me an abusive father, nor have I ever had the slightest desire to molest a child. I remember those things on purpose now because they are a testimony to what God can do in a broken life. That experience helped make me a compassionate leader and reminds me of why Jesus said, *"It would be better for him if a millstone were hung around his neck, and he were thrown into the sea, than that he should offend one of these little ones"* (Luke 17:2).

Now, about forgiveness: the Bible's teaching about forgiveness is pretty incredible. Jesus said, *"For if you forgive men their trespasses, your heavenly Father will also forgive you. But if you do not forgive men their trespasses, neither will your Father forgive your trespasses"* (Matthew 6:14–15). He also told a parable about a servant who was forgiven of an impossibly huge debt (like the sin-debt we owe to God) but refused to forgive

> "Blessed are the merciful, for they shall obtain mercy." (Matt. 5:7)

his neighbor of a few-dollars debt. Jesus said that, as a result, the unforgiving man was called to account for his own debt even though he and his family were ruined forever.

God demands that we forgive. I've found a reason for forgiving that may appeal even more to an outraged victim, though. After all, it's hard to accept that we should forgive an abuser just because "God said so." That should be a good enough reason for anyone, but I've personally experienced the emotions that say otherwise! So, try this on for size—*unless you forgive the abuser, you will never be able to put the abuse behind you.*

It's true: as long as you hold the abuser responsible for his actions, your sense of justice will keep the abuse active in your mind as unfinished business. You see, the enemy does his best to trap us coming and going—and our fallen natures cooperate far too easily! People stop drinking but start smoking. They stop smoking but start overeating. They swear off drinking coffee but start drinking cola. They break free from an abusive situation but become trapped in bitterness.

Only when you pardon the abuser—a pardon he doesn't deserve—will you be able to lay the issue to rest. *"Beloved, do not avenge yourselves, but rather give place to wrath; for it is written, 'Vengeance is Mine, I will repay,' says the Lord"* (Romans 12:19). It takes a lot of trust, but you have to believe that God will take care of what needs to be done. Once you get a grasp on this, it is very liberating. You can simply hand the abuser over to God and say, "Take care of this guy for me, okay?" Then you can forget about it because God is a completely righteous judge, and He will do what is best.

The Bible says that if you don't forgive, you won't be forgiven. Not only that, but you won't be free from the pain of your abuse, either. So you could leave an abusive situation, and wind up in an equally bad one. I have seen women do this time and time again. Because they left bad relationships without letting God clear their heads or heal their hearts, they went straight into the arms of other abusive men.

I have seen people do the same with churches, too. Sometimes a wounded person will go to a perfectly healthy church and take their wounds with them. Because of the bitterness inside, they flail around, trying to keep themselves "safe" and wind up hurting innocent people around them. I think this is why so many pastors say, "If you find the perfect church, don't join it—'cause you'll ruin it!" Sometimes we must deal with the mess inside our hearts before we can fix what goes on outside.

Authority Abusers

Don't misunderstand what it means to forgive. You cannot say that "it's okay" that someone abused you. It's not okay. What they did was wrong, no matter what good God wants to bring out of it. It was sin, and nothing you say or do can change that. You didn't cause them to sin, and their own circumstances cannot justify their actions. Sin is sin. Abuse is always abuse. You are releasing them from your personal judgement, but they still have to face God's. C. S. Lewis gave a splendid description of this mind-set in his book, *Mere Christianity*:

> For a long time I used to think this a silly, straw-splitting distinction: how could you hate what a man did and not hate the man? But years later it occurred to me that there was one man to whom I had been doing this all my life—namely myself. However much I might dislike my own cowardice or conceit or greed, I went on loving myself. There had never been the slightest difficulty about it. In fact the very reason why I hated the things was that I loved the man. Just because I loved myself, I was sorry to find that I was the sort of man who did those things. Consequently, Christianity does not want us to reduce by one atom the hatred we feel for cruelty and treachery. We ought to hate them. Not one word of what we have said about them needs to be unsaid. But it does want us to hate them in the same way in which we hate things in ourselves: being sorry that the man should have done such things, and hoping, if it is anyway possible, that somehow, sometime, somewhere he can be cured and made human again.

Step Two: Adjusting Your Life

"What?" I can hear someone asking, "My life has been turned inside out by an abusive leader. I don't want to *adjust!* I want to get back to normal!" I can understand that; but if you were the strong, insightful person that God designed you to be, how were you trapped by an authority abuser in the first place? Don't you believe God wants you to be able to see what's wrong in a situation like that and avoid it altogether?

If that's true, why would you want to go back to what you used to call "normal"? Yes, you need to be free from bitterness and pain. But should you refuse to learn anything or to grow? No. God wants to build you into a person you never knew you could be. He wants to show you your true self. He wants you to flourish under godly authority.

> God wants to show you your true self.

It may sound strange at first, but the process for building your new life is the same as for a former abuser. You must adopt a life of discipline so that you take in God's truth and grace on a daily basis. Chew over what the Word says about you.

> *You are not your own....For you were bought at a price; therefore glorify God in your body and in your spirit, which are God's.* (1 Corinthians 6:19–20)

> *Are not five sparrows sold for two copper coins? And not one of them is forgotten before God. But the very hairs of your head are all numbered. Do not fear therefore; you are of more value than many sparrows* (Luke 12:6–7)

> *Who shall separate us from the love of Christ? Shall tribulation, or distress, or persecution, or famine, or nakedness, or peril, or sword?....In all these things we are more than conquerors through Him who loved us. For I*

am persuaded that neither death nor life, nor angels nor principalities nor powers, nor things present nor things to come, nor height nor depth, nor any other created thing, shall be able to separate us from the love of God which is in Christ Jesus our Lord. (Romans 8:35–39)

Get used to making prayer a conversation with God. Don't be afraid to tell Him, "God, I'm asking for Your help, because I need it." You can't create the new you, and you can't force yourself to become stronger and wiser. But you can ask God for help with it. God promised, *"If any of you lacks wisdom, let him ask of God, who gives to all liberally and without reproach, and it will be given to him"* (James 1:5) Then He cautioned, *"But let him ask in faith, with no doubting, for he who doubts is like a wave of the sea driven and tossed by the wind"* (v. 6). Ask God and believe that He will supply the wisdom.

Be patient with yourself. You will make mistakes, so don't assume God didn't give you wisdom when you asked or that He never sent His grace to be your strength. Building a life is a process. Remember, though, you have a wonderful promise in His word: *"He who has begun a good work in you will complete it until the day of Jesus Christ"* (Philippians 1:6).

Step Three: Submitting to Godly Authority

As God began to heal me from the wounds I received at the hands of abusive leaders, I wasn't looking for an authority to submit to. I guess I must have known in the back of my head that I would need some kind of spiritual leadership or accountability some day, but I was simply focused on what God put right in front of me. Imagine my surprise, when one day God put in front of me authority figures I could trust and respect!

Restoration of Proper Authority

I don't think I'm in a place where I can tell you to run out and start hunting for someone to submit to. I do know God will want to set you under an authority that will bless and nurture the work He is doing in you, though, and He will provide such a person in His time. I also know that all believers need to be a part of a healthy, well-balanced church, and I do think you should make finding one a priority. Don't expect to find a perfect church; just look for one that houses God's presence and sincerely seeks to apply His truth to its community. Finding the right church may not be a quick process, but make sure you're not holding each place up to your own standards of what a church should be. Instead ask God whether what He is doing in you and what He is doing in that church makes the two of you a match.

When you find the place where you belong, you will have to submit yourself to the leadership. You don't have to abruptly throw yourself on the floor before your pastor. As you spend time in the church, however, he should be able to get to know you, get a feel for who you are, and have input into your life. You will have to trust again; but when your ultimate trust is in the Lord, you'll have the courage to give it a shot.

I believe that, eventually, you will *"be like a tree planted by the rivers of water, that brings forth its fruit in its season, whose leaf also shall not wither; and whatever [you do] shall prosper"* (Psalm 1:3). Your pastor (or other leader) will be like a skilled gardener, pruning your branches and watering the soil you're rooted in. By God's grace, authority will be at work once again.

Study and Discussion Guide

Chapter One

1. Like all evil, authority abuse is a _____ of something God intended to beautiful.

2. What is one word to describe this kind of evil?

_____

3. God takes authority abuse very seriously. What was the real punishment Jesus described for the wicked foreman in Matthew 24:44–55?

_____

_____

Chapter Two

1. True authority is _____ from above.

2. Who first set up the order of authority?

_____

3. What is authority for? _____

_____

4. Explain in your own words why authority is necessary in a world of free will.

_____

_____

_____

Chapter Three

1. Authority can be intoxicating. What kind of leaders are most at risk of being overcome by it?

_____

_____

2. In your own words, give two reasons that people abuse their authority.

_1)_ _____

_____

_2)_ _____

_____

Authority Abusers

Chapter Four

1. Give a simple definition for authority abuse:

_____

_____

2. List five ways to recognize authority abuse:

1) _____

2) _____

3) _____

4) _____

5) _____

(continued on next page)

3. Now, in your own words, explain your answers to question two.

_____

_____

_____

_____

_____

_____

_____

_____

_____

_____

_____

_____

_____

_____

_____

_____

Chapter Five

1. A biblical view of finances will teach you to:

Eat your _____ and sow your _____

2. What is your "bread"? _____

_____

What is your "seed"? _____

_____

3. Does God promise to make you wealthy?

_____

Chapter Six

1. Who has the first responsibility to keep an abusive leader out of the home?

_____

2. What is the simplest way to do this?

_____

_____

_____

3. Define in your own words what it means for a husband and wife to be "one flesh":

_____

_____

_____

_____

Chapter Seven

1. Does the Bible support the idea that a man should be "king" of his house?_____

2. Why does a husband have authority over his wife?

_____

_____

3. Is it ever right in God's sight to deprive your spouse of what he or she genuinely needs?

_____

Why or why not? _____

_____

Chapter Eight

1. Is godly authority democratic? _____

2. Why or why not? _____

_____

_____

3. Think about a situation in which you had trouble submitting to the authority over you. If you didn't deal with this problem, would it affect your ability to lead other people in a godly way? Why or why not?

_____

_____

_____

Chapter Nine

1. What does it mean to "medicate" yourself with God's Word and prayer?

_____

_____

2. What about forgiveness is hardest for you? What can you do to open your heart and allow God to love through you?

_____

_____

_____

_____

(continued on next page)

3. Explain how you can seek a life of discipline in order to discover the person God wants you to be. How can you personally apply this to your schedule?

_____

_____

_____

_____

_____

_____

_____

_____

_____

_____

Journal

What things did the Lord speak to you in each of these chapters? What changes will you need to make as a result of God's word to you? Write your thoughts in the following pages, making an entry for each chapter.

_____

_____

_____

_____

_____

_____

_____

_____

_____

_____

_____

_____

Authority Abusers

Journal

Authority Abusers

_____

_____

_____

_____

_____

_____

_____

_____

_____

_____

_____

_____

_____

_____

_____

_____

_____

_____

Journal ☩

Authority Abusers

_____

_____

_____

_____

_____

_____

_____

_____

_____

_____

_____

_____

_____

_____

_____

_____

_____

_____

_____

Journal

_____

_____

_____

_____

_____

_____

_____

_____

_____

_____

_____

_____

_____

_____

_____

_____

_____

_____

About the Author

Bishop George G. Bloomer is a native of Brooklyn, New York. After serving as an evangelist for fourteen years, Dr. Bloomer began pastoring in 1996. He is the founder and senior pastor of Bethel Family Worship Center in Durham, North Carolina, but continues to travel extensively—sharing with others his testimony of how the Lord delivered and set him free from a life of poverty, drug abuse, sexual abuse, and mental anguish. Where others may have lost their minds, committed suicide, or even been killed, the Lord graciously held tragedy at bay and Bishop Bloomer has now turned those negative experiences into a positive and remarkable ministry. He attributes this all to one amazing fact: "God had a plan for my life, and even during my span of lawlessness, the angels of the Lord were protecting me because the call of God was upon my life."

Dr. George Bloomer holds the degree of Doctor of Religious Arts in Christian Psychology and conducts many seminars dealing with relationships, finances, and stress management. He is also the founder of Young Witnesses for Christ, a youth evangelistic outreach ministry with several chapters on college campuses throughout the United States, and Bishop of C.L.U.R.T (Come Let Us Reason Together) International Assemblies, comprised of over 80 churches nationwide and abroad. His message is one of deliverance and of a hope that far exceeds the desperation and oppression of many silent sufferers.

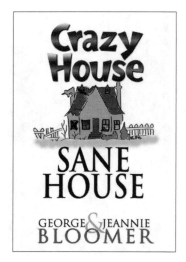